# Rational Economic Decisions and the Current Account in Kenya

GEOFFREY MWAU
*and*
JAGDISH HANDA

# Avebury

Aldershot • Brookfield USA • Hong Kong • Singapore • Sydney

Published by
Avebury
Ashgate Publishing Limited
Gower House
Croft Road
Aldershot
Hants GU11 3HR
England

Ashgate Publishing Company
Old Post Road
Brookfield
Vermont 05036
USA

**British Library Cataloguing in Publication Data**

Mwau, Geoffrey
    Rational Economic Decisions and the
    Current Account in Kenya. - (Making of
    Modern Africa Series)
    I. Title  II. Handa, Jagdish III. Series
    330.96762

ISBN 1 85972 236 9

**Library of Congress Catalog Card Number:** 95-78265

Printed and bound in Great Britain by
Ipswich Book Co. Ltd., Ipswich, Suffolk

# Contents

# Contents

# Preface

All African countries have experienced severe economic shocks to their economies since 1973. In spite of a variety of governmental policies adopted to cushion the impact of these shocks on the domestic economy, the virtually uniform experience of African countries (south of the Sahara) has been widening current account deficits and a slowdown in economic growth since 1973. This experience has brought about a resurgence of interest and research on the adjustment experiences of the African economies to external shocks and, in a wider context, has contributed to such research on the developing economies generally.

This book focuses on the central issue of whether the economic behaviour of the government and the private sector in developing economies can be adequately studied by the neoclassical models based on the assumption of rational, optimizing agents. To do this, it presents a theoretical and econometric application of the rational, optimizing neoclassical analysis, with appropriate modifications to incorporate certain core structural rigidities to the special case of the Kenyan economy. It examines the external shocks which have buffeted the Kenyan economy since 1973 and determines their impact, through governmental and private sector responses, on the current account. It finds that the modified neoclassical analysis is valid for the Kenyan context, and by inference, for the wider context of the developing countries generally. However, the book does not find sufficient support for the assumption of rational expectations in the context of a developing country such as Kenya.

At a more specific level, this book examines the relative contributions of the direct effects and the indirect effects on the current account which arise from the impact of external shocks to the economy. The direct effects arise from the optimal responses by both the private agents and the government.

*Preface*

The former depend upon the private agents' objective functions and the constraints on them. The latter operate through governmental policies intended to counteract the effects of the shock on the economy and depend on the government's objectives, subject to the relevant constraints on the structure of the economy. The indirect effect is that of the government policy response on private sector behaviour and the impact of this reaction on the current account.

This book finds that both of the economic agents - the government and the private sector - in Kenya are responsive to exogenous shocks as predicted by neoclassical economic theory, and that the assumption of a rigid structure of the economy is not valid. The government acts as a Stackleberg leader, with the private sector responding to the governmental policy responses to the external shocks. Hence, the government when setting its policies must not ignore the private sector's optimal reactions to those policies and the extent to which such reactions will nullify the intended results of its policies.

This book is based on:

Geoffrey Mwau. *Government and Private Sector Responses to External Shocks and their Effects on the Current Account: Evidence from Kenya, 1973-1988*. Ph.D. Dissertation. Montreal: McGill University, 1994.

We would like to thank Professor John Iton of McGill University, a supervisor of the dissertation on which this book is based. His guidance, criticism and comments on the dissertation were invaluable.

We are indebted to the *International Development Research Center* (IDRC) of Canada for providing Geoffrey with financial assistance to study at McGill University. We are also indebted to *les Fonds pour la Formation de Chercheurs et l'aide a la Recherche* of Quebec for financial research assistance.

At a personal level, we are grateful to Jeffrey Fine, Issa Omari and Aline Guay (all of IDRC) with whom Geoffrey interacted so closely during his years at McGill University, and to many other students and colleagues at McGill for their assistance and encouragement.

# About the authors

## Jagdish Handa

Jagdish Handa is Professor of Economics at McGill University in Montreal, Canada. He obtained his B.Sc. (Econ.) from the London School of Economics in 1962 and his Ph.D. from Johns Hopkins University in 1968. He has been at McGill University since 1966. He has published in a variety of fields in economics, including utility theory, risk aversion and portfolio selection, currency substitution, economics of developing countries and labour economics. His latest books are *Devaluation Policy and the Indian Economy* (jointly with Ashok Nigam) and *Discrimination, Retirement and Pensions*. His numerous articles have appeared in a number of journals and edited books.

## Geoffrey Mwau

Geoffrey Mwau did his studies in Kenya and Canada, completing his Ph.D. at McGill University in Montreal in 1994. Before returning to Kenya, he worked as an economist in the African Department of the International Monetary Fund during 1991-94. He has taught economics at the University of Nairobi. His research interests are in economic policy analysis, development macroeconomics, industrial development, and agricultural and economic resource economics. Currently, Dr. Mwau is involved in teaching, research and private consulting in economic policy and development issues in Kenya.

# 1  Introduction

A major point of contention in the economic literature on the developing economies is the extent to which the economic behaviour of the government and the private sector can be adequately studied by the neoclassical models based on the assumption of rational, optimizing agents. These models allow the main economic assumptions and theories of neoclassical economics to be applied to these economies and permit the rigorous evaluation of the policies pursued in these economies. They also allow an evaluation of the reasons for the successes and failures of these economies, and a comparison across countries. The alternative approaches to such models can be descriptive or theoretical analysis; even if it is theoretical, the theories may be *ad hoc* and very specific to the developing economy being studied. Further, in these alternative approaches, the economic agents are not always postulated to be rational and/or optimizing, but are often taken to operate in a particular context, with a particular structure of the economy and in line with local traditions and patterns of behaviour. These limit the generality of any findings of such studies.

Even in the applications of the neoclassical theories to the developing economies, the policy response of the government is often studied as if it was *ad hoc*, rather than being a rational response to the shocks to the economy. Further, the reaction of the private sector to these governmental policy responses may also not be modelled in the rational, optimizing manner.

This book is a study in the theoretical and econometric application of the rational, optimizing neoclassical analysis to the special case of the Kenyan economy. It attempts to determine whether such an analysis is valid for the Kenyan context, and by extension, for the wider context of the developing countries generally. However, we modify this analysis to incorporate many of

1

the distinctive structural aspects of the developing economies and to use the extended framework for testing. Within the Kenyan context, the focus is on the external shocks on the Kenyan economy and their impact, through governmental and private sector responses, on the current account.

Starting from the mid-1970s, developing countries have been subjected to severe external economic shocks that had adverse effects on their current account and economic performance in general. Some of these shocks were the terms of trade changes associated with fluctuations in the prices of main imports and exports; increases in the price of imported inputs; changes in the demand for exports (mainly associated with economic performance in industrial countries); and increases in their cost of borrowing, etc. To illustrate the extent of the shocks and their impact on the current account between 1973 and 1981, the terms of trade for non-oil producing developing countries deteriorated by about 2% per annum on average and the current account deficits deteriorated by about 3% per annum on average (Khan and Knight 1983).

In response to such shocks, many governments in the developing countries responded with macroeconomic policies aimed at restoring the balance of payments equilibrium and stimulating growth. While some developing countries succeeded in restoring macroeconomic equilibrium, others ended up with a worsening of the current account deficits and a further slowdown in economic performance. Virtually all African countries experienced widening current account deficits and a slowdown in economic growth (World Bank 1980; Gulhati and Yalamanchili 1988).

The mixed performance of these countries since 1973 have brought about a resurgence of interest in the adjustment experiences of the developing economies. In particular, many economic studies have focused on the quantitative effects of external shocks and government policies on the balance of payments and other macroeconomic variables. Several studies have also attempted to determine the relative importance of external and internal shocks in determining macroeconomic performance. Although these studies do make important contributions to the literature, many tend to suffer from one or several of the following limitations.

First, most of the models incorporate *ad hoc* behavioral relationships with little or no theoretical foundation. Second, they give inadequate attention to the role of expectations, even though rational expectations are now a common feature of the macroeconomic analysis in developing economies (Haque and Montiel 1989). Third, the methodology of many studies ignores the possibility that government policy responses may effect the behaviour of private agents, which in turn would have implications for the current account of the balance of payments and economic performance. They consider only the direct effects of the shocks that arise when the government and private sector respond to the shocks. However, rational economic agents would react to governmental policies, so that there would also be indirect effects, occurring through the impact of government policy responses on private sector behaviour.

Several studies of the current account based on the intertemporal optimizing behaviour of economic agents and forward looking expectations have been undertaken for several developed countries (for example, see Sachs 1981, 1982). Using such models, it is possible to derive the optimal responses of the private sector and the government to external shocks and from these, to derive their effects on the current account. Recently, Conway (1986, 1987) extended such an analysis to Turkey, a semi-industrialized country. Such studies have not been undertaken for developing countries.

This book extends the optimizing, rational expectations analysis to the general case of developing countries and tests its specific application by using Kenyan data for the period 1964-1988.[1] Among the objectives of this book are:

i. To test whether an intertemporal model of economic behaviour is relevant for the case of a developing economy like Kenya.

ii. To test the validity of the assumption of rational expectations in the context of a developing country such as Kenya.

iii. To test whether economic agents in Kenya are responsive to exogenous shocks as predicted by economic theory.

iv. To test if the private sector and the government react to each other's actions and to test for the pattern of this interaction.

Our model assumes that following an external shock, the rational behaviour of economic agents is to adjust their production and spending behaviour in an optimal manner. Depending on the degree of flexibility in the economy, the effect of this response is to reduce domestic absorption and thus improve the current account. At the same time, the government responds by undertaking policies which optimize its objectives given the shock. The private sector responds both directly to the external shock and to the governmental policies adopted in response to the shock. This theoretical framework is along the lines of Conway (1987) who has undertaken a similar study for Turkey, a semi-industrialized economy, but with our model specification and the estimating equations modified to capture key features of the Kenyan economy.

The reactions of both the government and the private sector are analyzed in the context of a game in which it is assumed that each agent takes the other's behaviour into account when formulating economic decisions. Two types of equilibria are examined: a Nash non-cooperative concurrent game; and a non-cooperative Stackleberg structure. Our results show that the interaction between the government and the private sector can be explained by the Stackleberg game structure where the government is the leader.

Our empirical results show that external shocks such as increases in the prices of imported inputs and exchange rate devaluation had a contractionary effect on the Kenyan economy: the producers responded to an increase in the price of imported inputs by reducing the demand for the inputs as well as the demand for labour. As predicted by the theory, both the government and private agents responded to the shocks in an attempt to maximize their objectives. The optimal responses of each agent were not necessarily in the other's interest since each agent reacted to counteract the undesirable effects of the other's behaviour. Also, both the direct and indirect effects of the shocks were found to be important in explaining the behaviour of the current account in Kenya.

This book is organized as follows. Chapter 2 provides a brief analysis of the main macroeconomic features of the Kenyan economy since 1964 and the role of government policy. Chapter 3 is a review of the literature. Chapter 4 develops a general theoretical framework and chapter 5 derives and estimates the behavioral relationships of the model. In chapter 6, we perform simulations to analyze the effects of various policy responses on the current account. Chapter 7 presents the summary and conclusions of the book.

## NOTES

1.      This period of study was determined by the availability of the data to us.

# 2 The Kenyan economy: macroeconomic developments, 1964-1988

## 2.1 Introduction

Kenya is an example of a small open developing economy. As in many other developing economies, agriculture is still the mainstay of the economy, contributing over 30% of total GDP over the period 1964-1988 (see table 2.2). However, the relative importance of this sector has declined from about 40% in 1968 to about 31% in 1988. A major characteristic of this sector is its dualistic nature. Small scale farmers operate alongside large scale commercially oriented farmers. Although occupying less than half the arable land, the small scale farmers contribute up to 60% of agricultural output and 75% of total employment (Vandermortelle 1986). Up to 85% of the population is either directly or indirectly dependent on agriculture.

The manufacturing sector has also grown significantly since independence. The share of manufacturing in total GDP increased from about 8% in 1968 to 13% in 1988. This was largely due to the import substitution industrialization policy adopted by the government soon after independence (Hazlewood 1979). From table 2.2, the share of manufacturing in GDP remained virtually constant at 13% from 1984 to 1988. Also, as indicated in table 2.5, consumer goods imports had declined to about 15% of total imports by 1980, indicating the end of the first stage of this import substitution process.

Another important feature of the economy is its degree of openness. This is characterized by a trade structure based on the import of intermediate and capital goods and the export of primary commodities. The degree of openness increased from 64% in 1964 to 76% in 1977 (Ikiara 1981). From table 2.5, it can be seen that the imports of intermediate and capital goods comprise over 50% of total imports for the entire period. The main exports are coffee, tea, and tourism which have contributed over 80% of Kenya's foreign exchange earnings. Their relative importance has been changing over time due to the fluctuating prices of coffee in the world market. The bulk of external trade is mainly with the western industrialized countries, with Britain, Germany, Japan and the USA taking over 80% of Kenya's exports.

Associated with the open nature of the economy is its vulnerability to external shocks. Changes in the terms of trade and exchange rate changes have a large influence on the balance of payments and thus on GDP. The oil price increases of 1973 and 1979 and the coffee boom of 1977 provide good examples of this, as indicated by Killick and Thorne (1981). Due to the open nature of the economy, economic developments in the western countries have a direct influence on economic growth in Kenya. Consequently, all the major recessions in the world economy have had a major effect on the performance of its economy.

The government has been directly involved in the economy mainly through public sector enterprises (PEs). The role of PEs in resource mobilization and production increased dramatically in the 1970s. This was a reflection of the then current thinking that they had a major role to play in the development process. There is evidence to show that some PEs were efficient and contributed to economic growth (Barbara 1987). Nevertheless, the Ndegwa Commission report of 1982 concluded that government intervention through PEs was a net burden on the economy (Ndegwa 1982). Since then, there has been an attempt to reduce the size of the public sector through divestiture, though with little success.

The rest of this chapter traces the macroeconomic developments in the country since independence, their influence on private sector behaviour and government policy. For the purposes of this chapter, it is convenient to distinguish between two main periods. The first one covers the post independence period from 1964 to 1973. This was a period of rapid economic growth with no major external shocks to the economy. The performance of the economy during this period is well documented in many studies including: King (1979), Maitha *et al* (1978), Killick (1981), Hazlewood (1979), and Bevan, Collier, and Gunning (1990). The main macroeconomic developments of this first period are summarized below.

The second period starts in 1974 and goes up to the end of the study period in 1988. Unlike the first period, the second one was characterized by very significant fluctuations in macroeconomic activity. A combination of external and internal factors contributed to the major fluctuations in economic growth, balance of payments, and GDP. There were also significant shifts in government policies, mainly in response to these shocks. Their implications for macroeconomic performance are discussed in the next section.

## 2.2 Macroeconomic performance, 1964-1973

The economy performed very well during 1964-1973, with the annual real GDP growth rate averaging about 6%. The per capita growth was relatively high, despite a rapid population growth rate of about 3.5%. The main contributing factors to the good economic performance were rapid agricultural expansion, especially small scale farming and growth in industrial output. Between 1964 and 1974, the manufacturing and agricultural sectors respectively grew by 9% and 4%. Also, the share of marketed output from small scale farmers increased by 10% (Killick 1981).

The economy's performance was not equally impressive in terms of income distribution and employment. As noted by the ILO (1972) and the World Bank (1975), the benefits of growth were not fairly distributed among all the income groups and employment growth could not match the rapid growth of the labour force. Inflation was very low, averaging 3.5% for the whole period. Despite a negative current account balance for the entire period, the overall balance of payments recorded a surplus which was mainly attributable to foreign capital inflows. In 1972, a combination of events resulted in a 'mini' balance of payments crisis.

In the absence of major exogenous shocks, government policy during 1964-1973 was focused on three main objectives: growth, equity and Africanisation of the economy. These objectives were specified in the *Sessional Paper No. 10 of 1965 on African Socialism and Its Application to Planning and Development*.

For the first eight years from 1964 to 1972, fiscal policy was well managed, enabling the authorities to realize a budget surplus in the current account up to 1969. A combination of strict expenditure controls, taxation and some borrowing from the banking system contributed to this remarkable fiscal performance. This was despite the demands placed on the government to Africanise the economy, with such Africanisation requiring an expansion of the civil service.

There was a major shift in fiscal policy in 1970 when a new Minister of Finance introduced an expansionary budget aimed at utilizing what were considered as idle resources in the economy. Government expenditures

7

increased by 17% in 1970. A similar expansionary budget in 1971 and a large increase in credit to the private sector led to an increase in the price level of 7% and a decline in foreign exchange reserves. The situation was worsened by an increase in the prices of imported goods, prompting immediate government response. Price and exchange controls were introduced and the 1972-1973 budget contained strict expenditure controls and a new sales tax.

Exchange rate policy was not actively used after independence. The Kenya shilling continued to be pegged at par with the pound sterling, as established in the colonial period by the East African Currency Board (EACB). This parity remained in effect after the Central Bank of Kenya was established in 1966. However, the shilling was effectively revalued when the Kenyan authorities elected not to follow the British government which devalued the pound sterling in 1967. It was felt that economic circumstances did not warrant a devaluation relative to the US dollar, as the balance of payments situation was healthy and a devaluation would have led to an increase in the cost of living (King 1979, p. 64).

The shilling continued its new fixed parity with the pound sterling until August 1971 when the United States government suspended its gold standard arrangements, thereby triggering a realignment of the exchange rates of major currencies. Initially, this realignment led to the appreciation of the shilling because the pound sterling, to which the shilling had been pegged, floated upwards against the US dollar. In october 1971, the three East African countries (i.e., Kenya, Uganda and Tanzania) decided to peg their currencies against the US dollar and maintained a fixed parity among their respective currencies. For the entire period up to 1973, the government followed a policy of a fixed exchange rate against the US dollar. Therefore, the exchange rate policy was not used to influence the behaviour of the economy for this period (King 1979).

The first two years after independence were a period of transition as far as monetary policy was concerned. Monetary matters were controlled from London but the East African Currency Board (EACB) was beginning to assume a more independent role. The initial emphasis was on monetary stability. The board intervened to keep interest rates lower when London rates rose sharply in 1964, creating an interest rate differential that together with a fixed exchange rate, caused an outflow of capital. Consequently, exchange controls were introduced in 1965 to check the capital outflow. There was a move towards a more independent policy when the EACB was disbanded and independent Central Banks were established by the three East African countries in 1966.

Even with an independent central bank, Kenya continued a policy of monetary conservatism, keeping interest rates low and stable. Government borrowing was restricted to K£12 million and the Central Bank of Kenya was required to keep a minimum of foreign exchange reserves equivalent to four months of imports. This helped to check the rate of growth of money supply. Monetary policy thus remained passive in the 1960s except when the Central Bank of Kenya intervened to restore the liquidity of the banking system following the appreciation of the shilling in 1967.

The passive role of monetary policy changed after 1971 when an expansionary fiscal policy and an expansion of private sector credit led to an increase in the money supply and a sharp decrease in reserves and higher inflation. A restrictive monetary policy in the form of credit controls was introduced in 1971. This was accompanied by a less expansionary fiscal policy announced in the budget speech of 1972. This speech included restrictions on the rate of growth of government spending and the introduction of a new sales tax.

The purpose of the governmental trade policy was to promote domestic industrialization and conserve foreign exchange. Protective measures included import licensing, quotas and, to some extent, tariffs. However, in this period, tariffs were not widely used because they were under the control of the East African Community at the time. The protective controls were widened as the process of import substitution and industrialization intensified. Between 1964 and 1970, the number of items that could only be imported under license increased from 64 to 228 (World Bank 1975).

The protective measures and a relatively more liberal foreign investment policy encouraged private foreign investment. The policies favoured sectors producing goods previously imported and were biased against exports. Consequently a pattern of industrialization emerged that was heavily protected and inefficient. It was biased against agriculture and exports in general. The main objective of price controls which were introduced at the beginning of the 1970s was to regulate profits in the manufacturing sector, in line with an incomes policy aimed at keeping wage growth below the rate of inflation.

## 2.3 Macroeconomic performance, 1973-1988

The period after 1973 was characterized by fluctuations in macroeconomic variables associated mainly with external factors. This instability in macroeconomic activity is evident from the behaviour of the major macroeconomic variables starting from 1973.

As table 2.1 shows, GDP growth averaged about 4% between 1974 and 1988, fluctuating between 1.5% in 1975 and 8.5% in 1977. This was in contrast to the pre-1973 period when the rate of growth averaged 6% and was fairly steady. The low growth years were 1974-1976 and 1982-1984, while the high growth years were 1977-1979. Performance for the rest of the years was around the average growth rate for the period. A high rate of population growth of 3.5%-4.1% led to a decline in per capita GDP growth.

The relatively poor performance of the economy was also reflected in the balance of payments developments which showed a similar pattern. Between 1974-1980, the current account balance averaged 10.5% of GDP, increasing to 13% in the period 1981-1988. Table 2.4 summarizes the balance of payments developments for the period. The current account including official transfers recorded very large deficits for most of the period. The worst years were: 1973-1974, 1978-1982, and the period after 1987. The best performance was in 1977 when a positive balance of K£11 million was recorded.

The rate of inflation was relatively high at double digit levels, averaging about 12% for the entire period (table 2.1). Inflation was relatively higher during 1974-75, averaging about 15%. Though remaining at double digit levels, the average rate was lower in 1983-1984 and 1986-88 when relatively low levels of inflation were reported.

A combination of factors contributed to the macroeconomic instability described above. The first oil shock of 1973 and poor weather in 1974 reduced growth to less than 2% in 1975 from 5.4% in 1973. Over the same period, inflation increased sharply from 8.9% in 1973 to 16% in 1975. The deficit in the current account of the balance of payments deteriorated from 5.1% of GDP in 1973 to 8.1% in 1975. The basic balance was negative for the years 1974 and 1975. The economic situation was worsened by the world recession of 1975. There was a recovery in 1976 which was strengthened by the increase in coffee and tea prices and good weather. The commodity boom reached its peak level in 1977, leading the economy to record a positive current account for the first time. By 1977, foreign exchange reserves stood at K£209 million, their highest level since independence. The rate of real GDP growth was very high at 8.5% for the same year. However, the rate of inflation remained high at 14.0%, mainly because of the monetization of the coffee boom earnings.

The quick recovery associated with the commodity boom was short lived and the economy began to deteriorate again by 1978. A decline in coffee and tea prices and the breakdown of the East African Community reduced both the volume and value of the major exports. The terms of trade worsened and the balance of payments started to deteriorate again. The second oil price shock of 1979 contributed to a further deterioration in the balance of payments so that by the beginning of the 1980s, the Kenyan economy was in serious balance of payments crisis.

Meanwhile, the limitations of the import substitution industrialization policy which had been predicted by the World Bank in 1975 began to be felt. The current account balance recorded a deficit equivalent to 12% of GDP in 1980, the highest since independence. Foreign exchange reserves fell to an equivalent of 1.1 months of imports in 1981 from an equivalent of 3.8% in 1977. Consequently, the manufacturing sector began to experience serious foreign exchange shortages.

By the beginning of the 1980s, serious disequilibria were beginning to emerge in the economy. Between 1980 and 1982, foreign exchange reserves were well below the statutory level of an amount equivalent to four months of imports (see table 2.1). The foreign exchange crisis forced the government to tighten import and foreign exchange controls. External borrowing increased substantially so that the foreign debt level rose to K£120 million in 1980 from K£98 million in 1979. The overall debt level increased from an average of K£80 million for the period 1973-1979 to an average of K£167 million between 1980 and 1988 (table 2.7). This borrowing was mainly from external sources and as a result, the debt service ratio rose from 12.1% in 1980 to 24% of GDP in 1983.

The poor economic situation in the 1980s was further worsened by the severe recession which hit the world economy at the time and the poor weather conditions during 1983-1984. This was reflected in a decline in output in 1983. The attempted coup of 1982 created serious political uncertainty that led to reduced capital inflows.

There was a slight improvement in the terms of trade in 1984 which was further strengthened by the 'mini' coffee boom of 1986 leading to an increase in foreign exchange reserves (tables 2.1 and 2.3). The terms of trade worsened after 1986 and foreign exchange reserves declined substantially by the end of the 1980s, reflecting a deteriorating current account balance. After a slowdown in 1986, the rate of inflation picked up in 1987, reaching 9.1% in 1988.

## 2.4 Exogenous shocks and government policy responses after 1973

External shocks began to have serious effects on the Kenyan economy after 1972. As noted in section 2.3 above, the oil shock of 1973 was the first major shock to hit the economy. There were subsequent oil shocks in 1979 and 1980. All the oil shocks had adverse effects on the balance of payments and economic growth. There were also two coffee (and to a lesser extent tea) price shocks in 1976 and 1986. The coffee and tea shocks had favourable effects on the balance of payments and growth but led to higher inflation.

Other exogenous shocks which hit the economy included the world recessions of 1974 and in the beginning of the 1980s; the drought years of 1974, 1982 and 1984; and the political instability associated with the attempted coup of 1982.

The government's policy responses were contained in a set of sessional papers starting in 1975. The policies reflected the government's perception of the impact of the shocks on the economy and whether the shocks were externally generated or not. There were short term policies intended to check the balance of payments deterioration, especially from the oil price shocks. The long term policies were focused on the long term growth of the economy. In general, the government seemed to be aware of the need for long term measures to change the structure of the economy but the implementation of those policies was unsuccessful (Bevan, Collier, and Gunning 1989).

One of the government's main policy responses to the deteriorating economic situation was external borrowing, mainly from the International Monetary Fund (IMF) and the World Bank (IBRD). There was also borrowing from private sources especially during the late the 1970s. This policy was pursued partly due to the perception that the shocks were temporary and were caused by external factors (Killick 1984).

The IMF loans were mainly for short term balance of payments support while IBRD loans tended to focus on the long term growth of the economy. As is common with the IMF and IBRD loans, the loans to Kenya required short term stabilization policies as the first step towards the elimination of the internal and external gaps largely associated with external shocks. The role of the policies was to control the growth of aggregate demand to make it consistent with aggregate supply. Also, supply side policies were required to stimulate aggregate supply and improve resource allocation. In the beginning of the 1980s, other donors started to base their lending on whether the country had agreed on a structural adjustment plan with the IMF and the IBRD. Most of the borrowing in the 1980s was therefore subject to some form of conditionality.

Prior to 1975, Kenya had drawn from IMF resources under the reserve facility and the oil facility amounts equal to K£19.4 million. In July of 1975, a new loan of K£29 million was approved by the IMF under the newly created Extended Fund Facility (EFF). This was a new line of credit designed to help those countries with special balance of payments difficulties and Kenya was the first country to benefit. Thereafter, five standby arrangements were approved in August 1979, October 1980, January 1982, March 1983, and February 1982. Each of these loans was approved with the understanding that the government would undertake the necessary policy measures to close the balance of payments gap, control inflation, stimulate output supply, and strengthen the long term growth of the economy. For each of the loans, detailed performance criteria were drawn, specifying clear targets for growth of the money supply, the budget deficit, and government borrowing from the Central Bank of Kenya. Other requirements were aimed at stimulating the growth of the traded goods sector. These included: trade liberalization; removal of quantitative restrictions; flexible interest rate policy; price decontrol; a more flexible exchange rate policy; and measures to reduce reliance on imported inputs.

Two Structural Adjustment Program (SAP) loans were also approved by the World Bank between 1979 and 1982. These loans were long term but required conditions similar to the IMF loans. There was a feeling that the IMF and the World Bank consulted each other to ensure consistency between the long term requirements of the World Bank loans and the short term IMF loans (Killick 1984). The World Bank loans, however, focused more on supply side policies and the long term path of the economy. These included policies to stimulate sectors with a high growth and export potential, especially agriculture.

The policy documents of the government indicate its acknowledgement of the need for structural adjustment. However, actual practice left a lot to be desired. The government reneged on its promises a number of times by exceeding the agreed government spending and credit limits. Consequently, none of the IMF programs negotiated between 1975 and 1982 was fully implemented.

The *Sessional Paper No. 10 of 1975 on Economic Policies and Prospects* laid down the policies undertaken in response to the 1973 oil crisis. The policies were very close to the IMF agreements suggesting that the government was willing to comply with the IMF requirements. A 15% devaluation and a 10% export subsidy towards the end of 1974 were seen as a response to the IMF and World Bank conditions.

The 1975 budget incorporated the major policy measures to be undertaken. Exports and imports were planned to grow at 8% and 2% respectively. The budget stayed within the limits agreed with the IMF and the rate of inflation was targeted to grow at half the rate of growth of import prices. Also, the government undertook a commitment to rationalize the tariff structure.

The initiative to stabilize the economy was discontinued in 1976 with

13

the onset of the coffee boom. The government did not feel the pressure to pursue the rather restrictive conditions and there was no urgent need. The changed attitude towards stabilization was reflected in the 1976 budget when, as a result of the boom, the government chose to exceed the spending and credit ceilings agreed with the IMF.

There was further fiscal expansion in 1977 with the Minister of Finance arguing that he was banking on unutilized resources in the economy. The budgets of 1978-1980 followed the trend set in 1976. The budget deficits remained relatively moderate because part of the expenditures were from increased revenues associated with the coffee boom. A political decision was made to pass all the benefits of the coffee boom to the private producers. This led to a substantial increase in money supply (see table 2.6). Net foreign assets increased by about six times between 1975 and 1977.

The consequences of an expansionary budget and the nonsterilization of reserves were high inflation and a larger current account deficit. During 1976-1979, inflation and the current account deficit averaged about 12.3% and 5.9% respectively. The current account changed from a surplus of K£16.4 million in 1977 to a deficit of K£256 million in 1978. The budget deficit was not very high because part of the government's expenditure was financed with increased revenues from the coffee boom. The budget deficit fell from K£85.5 million in 1976 to K£66.4 million in 1977 but increased to K£81.4 million in 1978, while the current account deficit doubled to K£150 million in 1979. It was financed largely by reserves which fell by K£35 million in 1976 and K£112 million in 1977. Further, the rate of inflation increased from 12.8% to 14%. There were some minimal measures undertaken to stabilize the economy but they were insufficient. In 1976 the government increased the reserve requirement ratio of commercial banks from 15% to 18% and increased it further to 20% in 1977. Import controls were relaxed in 1977 and a nominal export tax was introduced towards the end of the coffee boom. These measures were not enough to absorb the excess liquidity arising from the coffee boom. Consequently, money supply increased by about 49% during 1976-1979.

Up to the beginning of the 1980s, the government was not fully committed to stabilization and structural adjustment. This explains the failure to comply with the IMF and the World Bank programs and the lack of the government's own initiatives. As a result, the government's behaviour contributed to the internal and external disequilibria that emerged in the beginning of the 1980s. As noted earlier, these imbalances were exacerbated by the political uncertainty following the attempted coup in 1982 which caused financial instability and capital flight.

The government embarked on a structural adjustment plan and sought help from the IMF. By this time private capital inflows had dwindled following the debt crisis of the early 1980s. Long term capital inflows fell from K£147 million in 1980 to K£28 million in 1982. In 1985, there was an outflow inflow of K£21.8 million. Moreover, most foreign donors began to require that developing countries agree on a structural adjustment program with the IMF and the World Bank before they could obtain any financial assistance. The Kenya government therefore had very little room to manoeuvre.

A new standby arrangement of K£179.5 million was approved in March 1983 with similar conditions to the failed standby loan of 1982. The government was required to adhere strictly to a program of budget reduction, control of credit, reduction in domestic absorption, and a move towards a more flexible exchange rate policy. As a consequence of these measures, the budget deficit fell to K£192 million in 1983 from K£273 million in 1982. Also, real wages were allowed to fall for the first time. The IMF was satisfied with the implementation of the 1983 standby arrangement and as a result, another standby loan was approved in February of 1985. In December of the same year, Kenya was allowed to draw SDR 37.5 million under the compensating finance facility following increases in import costs. From 1983 on, the government seemed to be committed to structural adjustment. However, as can be seen from table 2.7, there was a further deterioration in the budget deficit.

The government maintained a fixed exchange rate policy until 1984 and regulated interest rates, contrary to advice from the IMF to liberalize them. Between 1974 and 1982, only two devaluations were undertaken and only under pressure from the IMF. A relatively more flexible exchange rate policy (in which small and more frequent adjustments of the exchange rate were undertaken) was adopted in 1984 and a program of price decontrol was initiated. Interest rates remained fixed at 5.6% from 1974 to 1979 and were increased to 6.4% in 1980. Given the high rate of inflation between 1974 and 1980 (see table 2.1), real interest rates were negative and the real exchange rate remained overvalued for the entire period.

Interest rates were not changed during 1980 but there was an upward adjustment in lending rates to 12.3% in 1981. They were increased to 13.8% in 1982 but declined to 13% the following year. There was a further reduction to 12% between 1984 and 1987 and then a 1% increase in 1988. Since 1981, the real rates have remained low but positive except for 1987 when the real rate was 5.9%.

## 2.5 The effects on private consumption and investment

Private sector behaviour was affected by the external shocks as well as government policies over the period. The extent to which both affected private sector behaviour is analyzed in chapters 5 and 6. From table 2.1, it can be seen that private consumption remained high throughout the period. Between 1973 and 1988, real private consumption as a percentage of GDP remained fairly steady, fluctuating slightly between 65% and 75%. However, real wages and therefore workers' consumption fell substantially after 1980.

Real private investment remained high between 1974 and 1981, averaging 13.8% of GDP. It was slightly higher at 16% of GDP during the coffee boom period of 1976-1978. This suggests that a larger proportion of private coffee earnings went to investment rather than to consumption. This is supported by the work of Gunning *et al* (1989). After 1981, there was a marked decline in real private investment. Between 1981 and 1988, the average ratio of private investment to GDP fell to 9%.

## 2.6 The behaviour of the current account

Table 2.8 shows the behaviour of the key components of the current account since 1973. Over the whole period, there were large fluctuations in net exports of goods and nonfactor services. Excluding the coffee boom years of 1976-1977 and 1986, the balance on net exports of goods and nonfactor services fluctuated along an increasing trend. Net factor payments increased steadily from 1973 to 1978 and fluctuated thereafter, with the lowest levels occurring during 1974-77. Their average level was K£-30 million from 1973 to 1978, K£-13 during 1979 to 1984 and K£-61.25 million during 1985-88. The positive figure for 1982 is due to the difficulties in transferring factor income abroad, largely associated with the unstable political situation during that time. Net interest payments show a steadily rising trend since 1973.

Except for the periods 1976-1977 and 1983-1986, net exports of goods and nonfactor services made the largest contribution to the current account deficit. Net factor payments were the second largest item until 1979 when they were overtaken by net interest payments. The fluctuations in net exports of goods and nonfactor services were largely due to fluctuations in external conditions and the policy responses undertaken by the government. The large increase in net interest payments reflected an increase in loans contracted at market rates and the maturing of loans borrowed during the 1970s. Moreover, the high world interest rates of the early 1980s contributed to the increase in the cost of external borrowing.

## Table 2.1

### Macroeconomic indicators, 1965-1988

|  | 1965 | 1966 | 1967 | 1968 | 1969 | 1970 |
|---|---|---|---|---|---|---|
| GDP Growth | 1.1 | 14.2 | 4.0 | 7.2 | 5.9 | 5.9 |
| Per Capita GDP | 72.6 | 80.0 | 81.6 | 84.8 | 86.8 | 89.2 |
| **Consumption (% GDP)** | | | | | | |
| Private | 85.4 | 81.7 | 81.5 | 80.4 | 77.1 | 77.0 |
| Public | 13.9 | 13.2 | 13.8 | 14.2 | 15.1 | 14.8 |
| **Investment (% GDP)** | | | | | | |
| Private | 14.4 | 14.5 | 16.7 | 16.4 | 17.0 | 20.2 |
| Public | 5.0 | 6.6 | 8.8 | 9.4 | 8.1 | 8.1 |
| **Current Account Deficit (% GDP)** | | | | | | |
|  | - | - | - | - | - | -3.1 |
| **Foreign Exchange Reserves (Months of Imports)** | | | | | | |
|  | - | - | - | - | - | -4.6 |
| Inflation (CPI) | 6.3 | 4.0 | 1.9 | 0.0 | 0.0 | 0.0 |

|  | 1971 | 1972 | 1973 | 1974 | 1975 | 1976 |
|---|---|---|---|---|---|---|
| GDP Growth | 4.5 | 6.1 | 5.4 | 2.6 | 1.5 | 3.8 |
| Per Capita GDP | 90.2 | 92.5 | 94.2 | 93.2 | 91.2 | 91.3 |
| **Consumption (% GDP)** | | | | | | |
| Private | 83.3 | 75.5 | 68.8 | 73.4 | 75.1 | 68.8 |
| Public | 16.2 | 16.4 | 16.2 | 17.1 | 18.9 | 18.8 |
| **Investment (% GDP)** | | | | | | |
| Private | 20.4 | 18.3 | 15.4 | 14.0 | 13.8 | 12.9 |
| Public | 12.2 | 11.2 | 12.1 | 10.7 | 9.6 | 9.4 |
| **Current Account Deficit (% GDP)** | | | | | | |
|  | -6.3 | -3.2 | -5.0 | -10.3 | -6.7 | -3.6 |
| **Foreign Exchange Reserves (Months of Imports)** | | | | | | |
|  | 2.9 | 3.5 | 3.2 | 1.8 | 1.6 | 2.6 |
| Inflation (CPI) | 3.8 | 8.9 | 8.1 | 15.9 | 16.0 | 12.8 |

## Table 2.1 (continued)

|  | 1977 | 1978 | 1979 | 1980 | 1981 | 1982 |
|---|---|---|---|---|---|---|
| GDP Growth | 8.5 | 5.5 | 5.7 | 3.1 | 5.3 | 3.2 |
| Per Capita GDP | 95.7 | 97.3 | 99.2 | 98.4 | 99.7 | 98.9 |
| **Consumption (% GDP )** |  |  |  |  |  |  |
| Private | 67.8 | 72.6 | 73.6 | 69.6 | 65.4 | 67.0 |
| Public | 20.2 | 21.7 | 21.8 | 21.5 | 19.3 | 18.6 |
| **Investment (% GDP)** |  |  |  |  |  |  |
| Private | 14.2 | 16.9 | 13.1 | 13.1 | 12.8 | 9.5 |
| Public | 10.7 | 10.6 | 11.2 | 21.5 | 11.0 | 9.5 |
| **Current Account Deficit (% GDP)** |  |  |  |  |  |  |
|  | 0.6 | -12.5 | -8.0 | -12.2 | -8.1 | -4.7 |
| **Foreign Exchange Reserves (Months of Imports)** |  |  |  |  |  |  |
|  | 3.8 | 1.8 | 3.4 | 1.9 | 1.1 | 1.2 |
| Inflation (CPI) | 14.0 | 14.5 | 8.0 | 13.0 | 11.5 | 21.0 |

|  | 1983 | 1984 | 1985 | 1986 | 1987 | 1988 |
|---|---|---|---|---|---|---|
| GDP Growth | 0.4 | 3.9 | 4.8 | 5.3 | 4.3 | 5.0 |
| Per Capita GDP | 95.5 | 95.3 | 96.0 | 97.0 | 97.2 | 98.2 |
| **Consumption (% GDP)** |  |  |  |  |  |  |
| Private | 65.6 | 68.4 | 64.9 | 70.4 | 72.9 | 74.2 |
| Public | 19.1 | 20.3 | 16.7 | 17.0 | 16.5 | 17.2 |
| **Investment (% GDP)** |  |  |  |  |  |  |
| Private | 9.1 | 8.8 | 8.7 | 8.9 | 9.8 | 9.3 |
| Public | 6.6 | 6.9 | 6.2 | 7.1 | 6.3 | 7.4 |
| **Current Account Deficit (% GDP)** |  |  |  |  |  |  |
|  | -0.8 | -2.0 | -1.8 | -0.5 | -6.2 | -5.4 |
| **Foreign Exchange Reserves (Months of Imports)** |  |  |  |  |  |  |
|  | 2.6 | 2.4 | 2.5 | 2.3 | 1.3 | 1.2 |
| Inflation (CPI) | 8.0 | 9.3 | 12.8 | 3.5 | 5.5 | 9.1 |

## Table 2.2

### Sectoral distribution of GDP: 1968-88
### (in percentages)

|      | Agriculture | Industry | Manufacturing | Services |
|------|-------------|----------|---------------|----------|
| 1968 | 40.0 | 15.6 | 8.3  | 44.5 |
| 1969 | 40.4 | 15.5 | 8.5  | 44.0 |
| 1970 | 39.4 | 15.5 | 8.6  | 45.1 |
| 1971 | 37.8 | 16.2 | 9.2  | 46.0 |
| 1972 | 36.3 | 20.5 | 10.6 | 43.2 |
| 1973 | 35.8 | 21.2 | 11.6 | 43.1 |
| 1974 | 34.5 | 21.1 | 12.0 | 44.4 |
| 1975 | 35.6 | 20.4 | 11.6 | 44.0 |
| 1976 | 35.5 | 19.8 | 11.2 | 44.7 |
| 1977 | 35.9 | 20.5 | 12.0 | 43.6 |
| 1978 | 35.0 | 21.4 | 12.7 | 43.6 |
| 1979 | 33.4 | 21.9 | 13.1 | 44.7 |
| 1980 | 32.5 | 22.2 | 13.2 | 45.3 |
| 1981 | 32.3 | 21.7 | 12.9 | 46.0 |
| 1982 | 34.3 | 20.7 | 12.6 | 45.0 |
| 1983 | 34.2 | 20.6 | 12.9 | 45.2 |
| 1984 | 32.7 | 20.9 | 13.3 | 46.4 |
| 1985 | 31.7 | 20.0 | 13.0 | 48.3 |
| 1986 | 31.5 | 19.7 | 13.1 | 48.8 |
| 1987 | 31.3 | 19.8 | 13.2 | 48.9 |
| 1988 | 31.1 | 19.9 | 13.3 | 49.0 |

Source: World Bank (1989). *World Tables*. Baltimore: Johns Hopkins University Press.

## Table 2.3

### Foreign trade indices

|  | Export Price Indices | | | Import Price Index | Terms of Trade Index |
|  | Non-Fuel | Fuel | Manufac-turing | Total |  |  |
|------|-------|-------|-------|-------|-------|-------|
| 1968 | 40.0 | 11.1 | 33.9 | 29.4 | 32.9 | 89.2 |
| 1969 | 41.4 | 11.1 | 43.5 | 28.8 | 34.4 | 83.9 |
| 1970 | 46.6 | 11.1 | 44.4 | 29.6 | 36.8 | 80.4 |
| 1971 | 44.3 | 14.5 | 42.6 | 32.0 | 44.6 | 71.6 |
| 1972 | 52.1 | 16.2 | 46.1 | 38.4 | 45.0 | 85.5 |
| 1973 | 63.5 | 23.1 | 67.0 | 53.8 | 58.8 | 91.4 |
| 1974 | 80.0 | 95.7 | 89.6 | 88.0 | 94.6 | 93.0 |
| 1975 | 72.2 | 93.3 | 87.0 | 80.5 | 95.1 | 84.6 |
| 1976 | 100.0 | 100.0 | 100.0 | 100.0 | 100.0 | 100.0 |
| 1977 | 150.5 | 109.4 | 97.4 | 133.3 | 111.7 | 119.2 |
| 1978 | 121.3 | 110.3 | 102.6 | 117.9 | 126.2 | 93.4 |
| 1979 | 134.4 | 159.0 | 113.9 | 139.1 | 148.8 | 93.5 |
| 1980 | 130.5 | 260.7 | 141.7 | 159.9 | 181.6 | 88.0 |
| 1981 | 112.6 | 293.2 | 145.2 | 152.3 | 189.3 | 80.5 |
| 1982 | 110.7 | 265.0 | 113.9 | 140.0 | 178.6 | 78.4 |
| 1983 | 116.9 | 241.1 | 105.1 | 140.3 | 171.9 | 81.6 |
| 1984 | 137.9 | 235.1 | 97.8 | 155.0 | 172.4 | 90.0 |
| 1985 | 113.7 | 228.2 | 97.8 | 134.9 | 166.8 | 80.9 |
| 1986 | 132.8 | 164.2 | 116.3 | 148.1 | 151.8 | 97.6 |
| 1987 | 103.2 | 174.7 | 116.2 | 123.1 | 173.4 | 71.0 |
| 1988 | 118.1 | 133.5 | 128.7 | 128.7 | 160.0 | 80.4 |

Sources: As in table 2.2.

## Table 2.4

### Balance of payments summary: 1973-1988
### (in K£ Million)

|                              | 1973  | 1974   | 1975  | 1976  | 1977   | 1978   |
|------------------------------|-------|--------|-------|-------|--------|--------|
| Current account              | -44.2 | -110.0 | -85.1 | -50.7 | 16.4   | -256.0 |
| Long term capital account    | 45.5  | 67.0   | 57.5  | 90.8  | 84.6   | 161.1  |
| Short term capital account   | 3.7   | 13.7   | 15.2  | -1.9  | 4.8    | 9.7    |
| Exceptional financing        | 0     | 0      | 1.8   | 1.0   | 3.4    | 7.7    |
| Change in reserves           | -32.9 | 28.8   | 20.5  | -35.3 | -111.6 | 76.0   |
| IMF Credit                   | 0     | 13.7   | 16.5  | 8.2   | -17.9  | 2.4    |
| Other                        | -2.9  | 15.0   | 4.0   | -43.5 | -93.7  | 73.6   |

|                              | 1979   | 1980   | 1981   | 1982   | 1983  |
|------------------------------|--------|--------|--------|--------|-------|
| Current account              | -178.7 | -365.5 | -253.4 | -166.4 | 32.0  |
| Long term capital account    | 137.2  | 146.8  | 88.0   | 28.3   | 92.5  |
| Short term capital account   | 81.6   | 45.9   | -3.7   | 25.9   | 5.7   |
| Exceptional financing        | 44.4   | 70.0   | 52.8   | 1.2    | 2.1   |
| Change in reserves           | -72.4  | 65.2   | 112.0  | 102.5  | -62.6 |
| IMF Credit                   | 27.0   | 21.3   | 12.3   | 81.4   | 61.9  |
| Other                        | -99.5  | 43.9   | 99.8   | 21.1   | 124.5 |

## Table 2.4 (continued)

|                       | 1984   | 1985   | 1986   | 1987   | 1988   |
|-----------------------|--------|--------|--------|--------|--------|
| Current account       | 90.9   | 92.6   | 31.4   | 409.6  | 404.3  |
| Long term capital     | 91.6   | -18.4  | 93.3   | 243.6  | 294.6  |
| Short term capital    | 37.7   | 35.9   | 14.3   | 117.0  | 41.5   |
| Exceptional financing | 2.2    | 3.3    | 1.9    | 1.1    | 1.2    |
| Change in reserves    | -27.3  | 81.8   | -73.3  | 69.2   | 46.5   |
| IMF Credit            | -11.1  | 39.2   | -94.2  | -98.9  | 66.8   |
| Other                 | -16.3  | 42.5   | 20.9   | 168.1  | 20.3   |

Sources: As in table 2.2

## Table 2.5

### End use analysis of imports: 1965-1988
### (in K£ Million)

| | Final Cons. | | Intermed. | Capital | Total |
|---|---|---|---|---|---|
| | Private | Govt. | Cons. | Formation | Imports |
| 1965 | 19.2 | 3.9 | 54.1 | 11.4 | 88.6 |
| 1966 | 22.4 | 6.4 | 59.9 | 17.2 | 99.4 |
| 1967 | 18.8 | 4.5 | 59.9 | 22.9 | 106.0 |
| 1968 | 21.6 | 4.9 | 64.5 | 19.4 | 110.4 |
| 1970 | 21.4 | 4.7 | 68.2 | 20.2 | 114.5 |
| 1971 | 26.8 | 5.8 | 82.2 | 27.6 | 142.3 |
| 1972 | 35.6 | 8.5 | 103.8 | 36.3 | 184.2 |
| 1973 | 33.6 | 8.6 | 104.8 | 42.6 | 184.8 |
| 1974 | 29.7 | 9.7 | 138.6 | 46.2 | 224.1 |
| 1975 | 35.3 | 15.8 | 253.8 | 46.8 | 351.6 |
| 1976 | 34.3 | 17.4 | 225.8 | 61.2 | 338.7 |
| 1977 | 45.6 | 22.2 | 238.7 | 71.7 | 378.2 |
| 1978 | 51.8 | 17.0 | 301.6 | 125.2 | 495.6 |
| 1979 | 59.2 | 30.0 | 325.7 | 172.2 | 415.0 |
| 1980 | 64.9 | 37.5 | 432.6 | 150.4 | 685.3 |
| 1981 | 95.1 | 61.7 | 740.3 | 162.8 | 1059.8 |
| 1982 | 98.8 | 84.0 | 527.7 | 146.4 | 857.0 |
| 1983 | 82.3 | 57.1 | 520.4 | 187.0 | 846.9 |
| 1984 | 87.6 | 53.1 | 499.2 | 176.6 | 816.5 |
| 1985 | 97.6 | 42.4 | 638.8 | 214.1 | 992.8 |
| 1986 | 99.3 | 42.0 | 648.0 | 216.0 | 1005.4 |
| 1987 | 162.3 | 61.9 | 763.6 | 410.9 | 1398.7 |
| 1988 | 160.8 | 84.6 | 856.6 | 396.5 | 1498.5 |

Source: Republic of Kenya. *Statistical Abstracts*. Nairobi: Government Printer, various years.

## Table 2.6

### Monetary survey: 1973-1988
### (in K£ Million)

| | 1973 | 1974 | 1975 | 1976 | 1977 | 1978 | 1979 | 1980 |
|---|---|---|---|---|---|---|---|---|
| Net Foreign Assets | 78 | 48 | 29 | 73 | 180 | 98 | 164 | 91 |
| Domestic Credit | 193 | 248 | 321 | 374 | 463 | 629 | 718 | 813 |
| Government: Net | 24 | 47 | 88 | 95 | 90 | 161 | 183 | 200 |
| Official Entities | 12 | 11 | 15 | 11 | 13 | 11 | 12 | 18 |
| Private Sector | 157 | 191 | 217 | 268 | 360 | 457 | 523 | 595 |
| Other Items: Net | 3 | 6 | 9 | 24 | 23 | 20 | 62 | 94 |

| | 1981 | 1982 | 1983 | 1984 | 1985 | 1986 | 1987 | 1988 |
|---|---|---|---|---|---|---|---|---|
| Net Foreign Assets | 7 | -108 | -51 | -19 | -99 | -21 | -108 | -183 |
| Domestic Credit | 1007 | 1281 | 1263 | 1403 | 1581 | 2001 | 2382 | 2495 |
| Government: Net | 339 | 535 | 436 | 479 | 518 | 778 | 996 | 919 |
| Official Entities | 17 | 28 | 58 | 78 | 88 | 90 | 178 | 173 |
| Private Sector | 651 | 718 | 769 | 847 | 975 | 1134 | 1208 | 1403 |
| Other Items: Net | 6 | 22 | 25 | 28 | 28 | 50 | 75 | 132 |

Source: IMF. *International Financial Statistics*. Washington, D.C., various years.

## Table 2.7

### Government finance and public debt: 1973-1988
### (in K£ Million)

|  | 1973 | 1974 | 1975 | 1976 | 1977 | 1978 | 1979 | 1980 |
|---|---|---|---|---|---|---|---|---|
| **Revenue** | | | | | | | | |
| Total | 141 | 181 | 217 | 256 | 308 | 459 | 492 | 591 |
| Current | 41 | 181 | 217 | 256 | 307 | 459 | 492 | 591 |
| Capital | 0 | 0 | 0 | 0 | 1 | 0 | 0 | 0 |
| **Expenditures** | | | | | | | | |
| Total | 171 | 197 | 259 | 308 | 362 | 496 | 597 | 681 |
| Current | 131 | 154 | 200 | 242 | 277 | 382 | 470 | 523 |
| Capital | 41 | 43 | 59 | 66 | 86 | 113 | 127 | 158 |
| **Grants** | 1 | 4 | 25 | 44 | 12 | 9 | 13 | 19 |
| **Overall Deficit** | | | | | | | | |
|  | 45 | 29 | 58 | 85 | 66 | 81 | 151 | 21 |
| **Total Debt** | | | | | | | | |
| Public | 24 | 30 | 34 | 43 | 57 | 73 | 98 | 120 |
| Private | 12 | 20 | 21 | 22 | 15 | 23 | 24 | 24 |

## Table 2.7 (continued)

| | 1981 | 1982 | 1983 | 1984 | 1985 | 1986 | 1987 | 1988 |
|---|---|---|---|---|---|---|---|---|
| **Revenue** | | | | | | | | |
| Total | 679 | 745 | 808 | 901 | 1009 | 1195 | 1380 | 1599 |
| Current | 678 | 744 | 808 | 901 | 1009 | 1195 | 1379 | 1598 |
| Capital | 1 | 1 | 0 | 0 | 0 | 0 | 0 | 0 |
| **Expenditures** | | | | | | | | |
| Total | 836 | 971 | 998 | 1101 | 1299 | 1431 | 1833 | 1998 |
| Current | 642 | 820 | 850 | 967 | 1089 | 1255 | 1500 | 1709 |
| Capital | 194 | 151 | 148 | 134 | 210 | 176 | 333 | 289 |
| **Grants** | 20 | 20 | 23 | 11 | 8 | 12 | 77 | 109 |
| **Overall Deficit** | 200 | 273 | 192 | 214 | 312 | 257 | 417 | 314 |
| **Total Debt** | | | | | | | | |
| Public | 127 | 139 | 143 | 146 | 170 | 203 | 237 | 221 |
| Private | 20 | 20 | 25 | 22 | 27 | 26 | 31 | 45 |

Source: World Bank (1989). *World Tables*. Baltimore: Johns Hopkins University Press.

Notes: Totals may not agree due to rounding. Also, total debt comprises long term debt only.

## Table 2.8

### Main current account components: 1973-88
### (in K£ Million)

| | 1973 | 1974 | 1975 | 1976 | 1977 | 1978 |
|---|---|---|---|---|---|---|
| Net exports of goods and services | | | | | | |
| | -19 | -85 | -65 | 1 | 49 | -218 |
| Net factor services | -26 | -21 | -17 | -38 | -40 | -38 |
| Net interest | -10 | -15 | -17 | -21 | -26 | -35 |

| | 1979 | 1980 | 1981 | 1982 | 1983 | 1984 |
|---|---|---|---|---|---|---|
| Net exports of goods and services | | | | | | |
| | -150 | -311 | -260 | -141 | -29 | -73 |
| Net factor services | -25 | -7 | -13 | 4 | -12 | -25 |
| Net interest | -45 | -65 | -78 | -102 | -111 | -120 |

| | 1985 | 1986 | 1987 | 1988 |
|---|---|---|---|---|
| Net exports of goods and services | | | | |
| | -50 | -4 | -356 | -409 |
| Net factor services | -54 | -33 | -41 | -117 |
| Net interest | -147 | -162 | -186 | -184 |

Source: World Bank (1990). *World Tables*. Baltimore: Johns Hopkins University Press.

# 3 The review of the literature

## 3.1 Introduction

The analyses of the macroeconomic adjustments to external shocks in developing countries are based mainly on the traditional approaches to the balance of payments analysis. Their main objective is to explain the role of external as well as internal factors in determining the key macroeconomic variables. These traditional approaches to the balance of payments adjustments have been criticized on theoretical grounds, especially with regard to the assumptions they make on the structural and institutional features of the developing countries. To deal with these criticisms, structuralist and Computable General Equilibrium (CGE) models have been developed as alternative approaches to the analysis of adjustment in the developing countries.

The next section reviews the traditional approaches to the balance of payments adjustment. Section 3 reviews the basic elements of structuralist and CGE models. Section 4 reviews the empirical approaches to analysing the current account and the empirical studies undertaken for Kenya.

## 3.2 The traditional approaches to the balance of payments adjustment

The traditional approaches to the balance of payments analysis are: the elasticities, the absorption and the monetary approaches to the balance of payments analysis. These approaches are critically reviewed in the following subsections.

### 3.2.1 The elasticities approach

The elasticities approach is based on the effects of devaluation on the relative prices of exportables and importables and thus on the effects of the devaluation on the current account. In its simplest form, it focuses on the elasticities of supply and demand for a country's exportables and importables. The conditions under which a devaluation can improve the current account and thus the balance of payments are derived in terms of these elasticities. These conditions were formalized as the Marshall-Lerner condition which shows that for a devaluation to improve the current account, the sum of the elasticities of demand for importables and exportables must exceed unity.

Mathematically, the simplest form of the Marshall-Lerner condition can be derived from the following equations:

$$X = X(P_m/P_X) \tag{3.1}$$

$$IM = IM(P_m/P_X, Y) \tag{3.2}$$

$$p = r.P^*_m/P_X = P_m/P_X \tag{3.3}$$

$$B = X(p) - p. IM(p, Y) \tag{3.4}$$

where:

| | |
|---|---|
| X | exportables |
| IM | importables |
| B | balance of trade (= X - IM) |
| Y | domestic valued added (GDP) |
| $P_X$ | price of exportables |
| $P_m$ | price of importables |
| r | nominal exchange rate defined as the domestic price of a unit of foreign currency |
| p | terms of trade. |

The superscript * denotes the respective foreign price.

We assume an economy specialized in the production of exportables and facing a perfectly elastic supply of imports. This implies that a devaluation raises the relative price of imports.

Equations (3.1) and (3.2) define the demand functions for exportables and importables respectively, and equation (3.3) defines the terms of trade or the relative price of domestic goods in terms of importables. Given domestic value added, the terms of trade determine how domestic expenditure is distributed between domestic and foreign goods. Equation (3.4) defines the trade balance (B) as the difference between the value of exports and the value of imports.

Differentiating equation (3.4) with respect to p gives:

$$\partial B/\partial p = \partial X/\partial p - p.\partial IM/\partial p - IM \qquad (3.5)$$

Equation (3.5) can be rewritten as:

$$\partial B/\partial p = \eta_x. X/p + \eta_m. IM - IM \qquad (3.6)$$

where:

$$\eta_x = (\partial X/\partial p) (p/X)$$

$$\eta_m = -(\partial IM/\partial p) (p/IM)$$

$\eta_x$ and $\eta_m$ are respectively the elasticities of the foreign demand for exportables and the domestic demand for importables. Assuming an initial trade balance in equilibrium implies that $(X/p)=IM$. Hence equation (3.6) reduces to:

$$\partial B/\partial p = (\eta_x + \eta_m - 1).IM \qquad (3.7)$$

which implies that $\partial B/\partial p > 0$ if and only if $(\eta_x + \eta_m) > 0$. This is the Marshall-Lerner condition which constitutes the basic version of the elasticities approach.

The elasticities approach has a number of weaknesses which especially limit its application to developing countries. First, the simple Marshall-Lerner result assumes an economy with full price flexibility, full employment, and an initial trade balance equilibrium. This ignores the fact that devaluation is usually undertaken to correct trade imbalances. Also, in the absence of full employment, a devaluation can generate income effects which may cause a deterioration of the current account. Second, the elasticities approach is based on a partial equilibrium framework that does not take into account the inter-relationships in all the markets. The nontraded goods sector and the real exchange rate issues are not treated in this approach. The assumption of independent markets for exportables and importables implicitly assumes that the cross price elasticities are equal to zero. In addition, this implies that

30

nominal and real devaluations are identical since the price of exportables is independent of external factors. However, recent studies in developing countries have shown that a devaluation is likely to cause the domestic price level to increase, and thus eliminate the relative price change which is crucial to stimulating an increase in exports (Agenor 1991).

Dornbusch (1975) showed that the elasticities approach can be easily extended to a framework which incorporates the general equilibrium features missing in its basic version. He shows that when home goods are included in the model, a devaluation may not improve the trade balance account unless there is a conscious policy to reduce domestic absorption. The argument is as follows: a devaluation increases the price of exportables forcing consumers to substitute home goods for exportables. This substitution causes the price of domestic goods to increase and therefore eliminates the relative price change between exportables and home goods. To prevent this, there must be supporting fiscal and monetary policies to reduce absorption.

### 3.2.2 *The absorption approach*

The absorption approach focuses on the income effects of devaluation. It was developed by Alexander (1952) who showed that a country's foreign trade surplus depends on the extent to which domestic output supply exceeds domestic absorption. Denote domestic output supply by Y and domestic absorption by A, where:

$$A = C^p + I^p + G$$

The current account surplus B (= X-IM) can be expressed as:

$$B = Y - A$$

$$= Y - C^p - I^p - G \tag{3.8}$$

where:

| | |
|---|---|
| A | domestic absorption (C + I + G) |
| $C^p$ | private consumption |
| $I^p$ | private investment |
| G | government expenditures |

Denoting total saving as S = Y - C, equation (3.8) can be rewritten as:

$$B = S - I \tag{3.9}$$

where:

$$S = S^p + S^g$$

$$C = C^p + C^g$$

$$I = I^p + I^g$$

The superscripts p and g represent 'private' and 'government' respectively.

Equation (3.9) brings out a key relationship in Keynesian models of income determination. It integrates the relationship between the current account and the difference between saving and investment. Modern theories of the current account determination take off from this basic relationship. They extend this static relationship to an intertemporal framework and use it to analyze current account dynamics. Recent studies using the dynamic intertemporal framework include: Svenson and Razin (1983), Sachs (1981, 1982), Haque and Montiel (1991).

As presented in equations (3.8) and (3.9), the absorption approach is essentially a rearrangement of the standard Keynesian income-expenditure identity. Alexander extended this by showing how devaluation affects the trade balance through its influence on absorption. Defining the current account of the balance of payments as the excess of income over expenditure, he argued that for a devaluation to improve the current account, it must have an impact on at least income or absorption.

The main conclusion of the absorption approach is that to improve the current account, a devaluation must generate expenditure switching and expenditure reducing effects. For expenditure switching to occur, the elasticities must be 'sufficiently' high. Expenditure reduction occurs through changes in real income. The role of government policy is to facilitate the expenditure mechanisms.

Unlike the elasticities approach, the absorption approach incorporates general equilibrium features and allows for the existence of nontradable goods. However, its focus only on income effects ignores the relative price effects emphasized by the elasticities approach. As mentioned earlier, Dornbusch has shown that the two approaches can be integrated to produce a Keynesian type model of income determination. Even in this integrated form, the elasticities and the absorption approaches do not consider the inflationary effects of devaluation. Their focus on the current account downplays the importance of the capital account in the analysis of the balance of payments. Moreover, the two approaches do not consider the role of money in the determination of the balance of payments.

### 3.2.3 The monetary approach

The origins of the monetary approach to the balance of payments are associated with the writings of David Hume during the eighteenth century and the development of the quantity theory of money. In its modern form, the approach is closely linked to the work of Polak (1957) and other economists who worked at the IMF in the 1950s. It was further formalized by a group of economists from the University of Chicago under the leadership of Harry Johnson and Robert Mundell (see Johnson 1958; Mundell 1960).

The main argument of the monetary approach is that the balance of payments determination is essentially a monetary phenomenon. A balance of payments disequilibrium (i.e., a deficit or surplus) would arise if there is a disequilibrium in the demand for and supply of money. For example, with an excess supply of money, agents would want to rid themselves of the excess cash balances. This means that in a system of fixed exchange rates, agents will tend to substitute the excess cash for goods and bonds, some of which are foreign. Hence, an excess supply of money will lead to a decline in reserves when part of the excess money supply is spent on imports.

In its simplest form, the theory can be derived from the following identities:

$$M = F + D \tag{3.10}$$

$$F^{\#} = M^{\#} - D^{\#} \tag{3.11}$$

$$F^{\#} = B + \kappa \tag{3.12}$$

where:

| | |
|---|---|
| M | stock of money |
| F | total net foreign assets |
| D | total net domestic assets of the domestic financial system |
| B | current account of the balance of payments |
| $\kappa$ | capital account of the balance of payments |

The superscript $\#$ over a variable represents its partial derivative with respect to time.

Equation (3.10) represents the basic equilibrium identity in the money market. It defines the money stock in the economy as the sum of net foreign assets and net domestic assets. Equation (3.11) is obtained by differentiating (3.10) with respect to time. It specifies that the change in net foreign assets - which is the change in net foreign reserves - is equal to the difference between the change in the money stock (or the flow demand for money) and the domestic component of money supply (i.e., net domestic assets).

Equation (3.12) represents equilibrium in the balance of payments. The change in net foreign assets is expressed as the sum of the current and the capital accounts. We assume in the following an open economy with a fixed exchange rate.

From equation (3.11), reserves will decrease (increase) if the domestic money supply (credit creation) exceeds domestic money demand. Moreover, from equation (3.12), a balance of payments deficit (surplus) will be reflected in a decline (build up) in reserves. It follows that an increase in credit creation will lead to a decline in reserves, and hence a worsening of the balance of payments. In this form, a balance of payments deficit is seen as the way in which agents dispose of excess money in a system of fixed exchange rates.

The relationship between the monetary approach and the other approaches (i.e., the elasticities and the absorption approaches) can be derived from the following national income identity:

$$Y = A + X - IM \tag{3.13}$$

The current account is defined by:

$$B = X - IM \tag{3.14}$$

Equations (3.13) and (3.14) imply that:

$$B = Y - A \tag{3.15}$$

Combining (3.11) to (3.15) and setting $\kappa = 0$, the following relationships are obtained:

$$F^{\#} = B = X - IM = M^{\#} - D^{\#} = Y - A \tag{3.16}$$

The relationships in equation (3.16) show that the three approaches are similar *ex post* if $\kappa = 0$. Setting $\kappa = 0$ is a simplification which assumes that, with the capital account in equilibrium, changes in net exports will be

34

translated to changes in net foreign reserves. Other implications of the approach are: a country with a fixed exchange rate policy cannot maintain an independent monetary policy, and a devaluation or a change in tariffs or quotas can at best have short term consequences.

The applicability of the monetary approach in developing countries is questionable and this has made it a focus of criticism. Several assumptions are implicit in the approach. First, it assumes a long run situation with fully flexible prices. Second, only points of equilibrium are considered and as a result the dynamics of short run adjustment are ignored. Third, it is assumed that the demand for money is stable and that the money market clears instantaneously with no transactions costs. Consequently, real effects that are important in the other two approaches are ignored. As argued by Hallwood and MacDonald (1986), these assumptions do not represent the reality in many developing countries.

## 3.3 Structuralist and Computable General Equilibrium models

A common feature in all structuralist and CGE models is their recognition of sectoral interdependence and the role of relative price changes in determining resource allocation. Although sharing certain features, these two types of models differ in the way they model economic behaviour and the assumptions they make about key behavioral parameters.

### 3.3.1 The structuralist models

The structuralist approach attempts to explain why, contrary to the traditional view, orthodox stabilization policies may not work in developing countries as predicted. An historical exposition of the formalization of this approach is available in Nigam and Handa (1990). Here, we review the key elements of the formal model. One of the main arguments of the structuralist approach is that a devaluation may not induce the expenditure reducing and switching effects predicted by the orthodox models of balance of payments analysis. Their explanation is that most developing countries face low elasticities of demand and supply and other structural rigidities that prevent the appropriate adjustments from occurring. Consequently, a devaluation may lead to a worsening of the current account. Empirical evidence, however, shows that there are often adequate supply and demand responses (see Khan and Knight 1983; Buffie 1989).

A second argument is that devaluation has contractionary effects which operate on output through the demand side. Devaluation redistributes income from low savers to high savers (especially from workers to capitalists) and in the process reduces domestic absorption. A formal explanation was provided by Krugman and Taylor (1978). Barbone and Rivera-Batiz (1987) showed that in economies dependent on foreign investment, part of the income redistributed to capitalists is repatriated. Hence, a devaluation can be contractionary even when the various income groups have the same marginal propensity to consume.

On the supply side, devaluation raises the prices of imported inputs and this has both contractionary and inflationary effects. Given the heavy dependence of developing countries on imported inputs, there is compelling support for this explanation. Taylor (1983) and Buffie (1989) report that the effect of devaluation through this channel is contractionary. The basic issue is whether the positive benefits of devaluation through expenditure reducing and switching are outweighed by the negative effects. Agenor (1991) has shown that empirical evidence on this issue is inconclusive.

Another supply side effect operates through high interest rates caused by a restrictive monetary policy. Bruno (1979) has shown that high interest rates increase the cost of working capital. At the same time, a devaluation increases the need for working capital by increasing the cost of imported inputs. Hence, a devaluation and a restrictive monetary policy may combine to cause a contractionary effect.

Although structural approaches have some validity, they suffer from certain weaknesses. The main weakness is that their behavioral equations are not based on optimization by economic agents, but rest on *ad hoc* assumptions regarding economic behaviour. Also, the empirical evidence in favour of them is inconclusive.

### 3.3.2 Computable General Equilibrium models

Computable General Equilibrium Models (CGE) models are founded on the Walrasian general equilibrium analysis and the neoclassical principles of optimization. Economic behaviour is modeled as an outcome of decentralized decision making by consumers and producers. The models assume a perfectly flexible price mechanism where prices adjust to equate supply and demand in all markets.

Some of the modifications to the above framework include the introduction of market imperfections in the goods, labour, money and foreign exchange markets; and appropriate assumptions about substitution mechanisms between labour and capital, between imports and domestic goods, and between exports and domestic sales. These are generally incorporated in the model by exogenously imposing structural rigidities such as fixed exchange rates, fixed wages, and zero elasticities of substitution.

A desirable feature of CGE is that their demand and supply functions are derived from optimization behaviour. Also, they recognize the interdependence of markets and the implications this has for policy interdependence. The CGE models can be disaggregated to as many sectors as the data permit and depending on need. However, certain limitations still remain in their applications to developing countries.

The manner in which these models often take market imperfections into account is simplistic. The demand and supply functions need to be derived from an optimization procedure where these imperfections are treated as extra constraints. This may, however, lead to increased computational problems. Even in the absence of market imperfections, the models assume structurally invariant parameters. This has serious consequences for their application in policy issues. Another limitation is that no account is taken of the intertemporal nature of many economic decisions.

A somewhat more sophisticated group of models attempts to eliminate most of the above limitations of the CGE models. Economic behaviour in the former is then derived from the optimization of objective functions by all economic agents including the government (see e.g. Sachs 1981, 1982; Bruno and Sachs 1985). Some of the studies along these lines also introduce intertemporal optimization and therefore bring to the foreground the issue of expectations formation mechanisms. These models have been applied in simulation exercises for developed economies and the results have been generally reasonable. However, no decomposition analysis of the current account based on such models has been undertaken.

Further, the theoretical complexity of these models makes their econometric estimation difficult without reliance on some very simplifying assumptions. For example, most of the models assume a representative producer and consumer to simplify the analysis. Blinder (1985) has pointed out that this ignores distributional considerations.

## 3.4 Empirical approaches to decomposing the current account

The empirical methods used to analyze the effects of external shocks on the current account are based on one or another of the above theoretical models. The existing studies in the literature have tended to explain the persistence of current deficits in developing countries by reference to two main factors: exogenous factors beyond the countries' control and inappropriate government policies. The empirical models have tried to decompose the current account deficits into these contributing factors.This section reviews the literature on this decomposition.

The technique developed by Balassa (1980a, 1980b, 1982) has been widely applied in analysing structural adjustment experiences in developing countries. Other studies using this technique include Balassa and McCarthy (1984) and Balassa (1984, 1989). Although no formal specification of a model for this technique is available, an underlying framework can be postulated from the structural parameters used in the approach.

The above studies analyze how developing countries responded to external shocks during the 1973-1978 and 1978-1983 periods. Three main types of shocks are identified for this period: terms of trade effects associated largely with increases of oil prices; export volume effects resulting mainly from recession in industrial countries; and the effects of the increase in interest rates in world financial markets in the early 1980s. Associated with these external shocks are the following types of policy responses: increased reliance on external borrowing, increased export promotion and/or import substitution; and macroeconomic policies such as fiscal, monetary, and exchange rate policies.

The methodology in the above studies involves a quantitative estimation of the balance of payments effects of the external shocks and the contribution of each of the policy responses. To estimate the balance of payments effects of a particular shock, a scenario is postulated which would have prevailed in the absence of the shock and is compared with the actual outcome. The terms of trade effects are calculated as the difference between the values of exports and imports at current prices and their values at constant prices in a chosen base year. They are further decomposed into a pure terms of trade effect and an 'unbalanced trade effect'. The pure terms of trade effect is calculated assuming that the balance of trade at base year values was in equilibrium while the 'unbalanced trade effect' measures the effects of a rise in import prices on the balance of trade surplus or deficit at base year prices.

The difference between the trend values of exports and a hypothetical path of export values is used to measure the effects of the slowdown in world trade (export volume effects). The trend value is calculated on the assumption that the export shares of some selected exports remained at the base year levels. The hypothetical path is derived assuming that the import shares of the same selected exports remained at the base year levels. The interest rate effects are computed as the difference between actual interest payments and the payments which would have prevailed if interest rates had remained at the base year levels.

A similar approach is used to estimate the balance of payments effects of adjustment policies. The difference between the merchandise trade balance at current prices and the trade balance based on the trend flows of exports and imports at constant prices is used to estimate additional net external financing. Export promotion effects are computed as the change in the country's base year exports shares. Import substitution effects are calculated as the savings in imports associated with a decline in the elasticity of import demand compared with the actual imports for the period. Macroeconomic effects are computed as the difference between the actual growth rate of GNP and the growth rate of GNP assuming unchanged income elasticities of import demand. The actual definitions and formulas used for all the computations are found in Balassa (1981, 1982).

The findings based on the above methodology share certain broad similarities. First, the countries are classified as either outward or inward oriented depending on whether, on the basis of the assumed policies, they tended to stimulate exports or import substitution respectively. This classification, although somewhat arbitrary, was supported by econometric studies where initial trade orientation and policy responses to external shocks were used as separate variables (see Balassa 1984, p.971).

Second, outward oriented countries seemed to suffer larger external shocks. These would limit their reliance on external financing, thereby causing a temporary decline in growth. However, the outward oriented policies of these countries increased exports and stimulated growth in the long term. Inward oriented countries postponed adjustment by relying on increased external borrowing which increased debt burdens. Also, their import substitution policies were biased against exports and did not help to alleviate the balance of payments deficits. These findings were supported by correlation results between the degree of outward/inward orientation and economic performance. There was no observed correlation between the magnitude of the shocks and the strength of the policy undertaken.

Balassa's methodology, though convenient in terms of computation and data requirements, has a number of limitations. First, its partial equilibrium nature ignores interactions among markets and this raises questions regarding the validity of the estimated coefficients. This is a serious limitation given the interdependent nature of many policies. The effects of policy responses to the balance of payments add to the balance of payments effects of the external shocks. This implies that the balance of payments effects are at least partly explained by the policies undertaken. Another limitation of this methodology is that no attempt is made to distinguish between permanent and temporary shocks. Further, the effects of the policy responses cannot be separated from the autonomous policies undertaken by the governments which may themselves constitute a shock. Regarding this limitation, Conway (1987) points out that structural adjustment is not properly captured in the models because the direct effects of external shocks cannot be clearly distinguished from the indirect effects through government policy responses.

Mitra (1984) extended Balassa's methodology by explicitly incorporating the underlying structural interrelationships of 34 developing countries in his model. He focused on the following adjustment responses to balance of payments effects of exogenous shocks: trade responses (export promotion and import substitution); domestic resource mobilization (both public and private sector savings); investment slowdown and additional external financing. Using data for each of the 34 developing countries, he estimated a macroeconomic model over the period 1963-1981, with a structural break in 1973. This represented the 'actual' behaviour of the economy over the period. The models were re-estimated assuming that there was no structural change to obtain a 'counterfactual' path of the economy. The actual and the counterfactual paths were then compared to identify the balance of payments effects of the policy responses. The trade response was attributed to expenditure and output switching policies; resource mobilization was associated with expenditure reduction; while investment reduction and increased external borrowing were attributed to delayed adjustment.

Comparing the results for the industrial countries in the group, Mitra identified four patterns of structural adjustment. One group of countries responded by increasing exports and public resource mobilization. The second group responded by either increasing exports or public resource mobilization. The third group undertook import substitution and reduced resource mobilization. The fourth group responded with increased external financing and some insignificant domestic adjustment. Also, some countries benefited from external economic events which reduced the need for adjustment.

Mitra's findings suggest that for most of the countries, both internal and external shocks were important in explaining balance of payments changes. His methodology, however, retains most of the weaknesses of Balassa's method. His model is not derived from the optimizing behaviour of economic agents and he still retains a similar set of invariant structural parameters. The model does not, therefore, pass the Lucas critique of econometric policy evaluation (Lucas 1976).

Another common method for analysing the current account in developing countries involves the use of CGE models discussed above. Recent studies applying these models to developing countries include: Robinson (1989) and Lewis and Urata (1984). As noted earlier, these models have been modified to incorporate the salient features of developing countries which are not captured in the standard formulation of the CGE models.

To evaluate the impact of exogenous shocks and the resulting policy responses, these modified CGE models use the procedure described by Conway (1987). According to the procedure, a base line 'reference' solution is generated which simulates how the economy would have performed in the absence of unfavourable external shocks. Another experiment is performed where the economy is assumed to be adversely affected by external factors but no changes in government policy are allowed. This provides a quantitative estimation of the balance of payments effects of external shocks. In the next step, experiments are performed where different combinations of policies are allowed and their impact on the economy are examined. Comparing the resulting scenarios provides an indication of the extent to which different policies contribute to adjustment.

Conway used the above methodology to analyze structural adjustment policies in Turkey, a semi-industrialized country. He developed a macroeconomic model which retains the intertemporal optimization framework and is still amenable to econometric estimation. His model provides a solid extension of the literature in several directions. One, he introduces two private economic agents (capital owners and labour) whose objectives differ from those of the government. This allows some distributional considerations to be incorporated in the analysis. The interactions of the private agents and the government and their different objectives are captured in a game theoretic framework. This provides a useful way of separating the direct impact of external shocks on private sector decisions from the indirect effects through government policy responses. This is a major improvement over the previous studies which were unable to make this distinction.

Conway's findings for Turkey for the period 1963-80 suggest that the behaviour of the Turkish economy is an outcome of an intertemporal game between the government and the private sector. He also found that the supply side considerations - e.g., the importance of imported inputs in the production process - are important in the Turkish case.

The results of Conway's decomposition analysis suggest that the direct effects of exogenous shocks led to reduced productive activity and aggregate investment. The policy induced effects led to increased productive capacity, investment and a worsening of the balance of payments. Also, the increased economic activity saw an expansion of government involvement in the economy. Theoretically, Conway's methodology is among the best available in the literature. It is solidly founded on the intertemporal optimizing principles and it is amenable to empirical estimation. Moreover, its results for Turkey are an indication that it could be useful for analysing adjustment problems of other developing countries.

This book uses a similar framework to analyze the structural adjustment experience in Kenya for the period 1973-1988. Conway's basic framework is being retained but the estimating equations have been modified to incorporate salient features of the Kenyan economy.

## 3.5 Empirical studies on Kenya

The existing empirical studies on Kenya consist of both single equation studies and large scale macroeconomic models. The latter focus mainly on the relative importance of internal and external factors in explaining macroeconomic disequilibrium in the economy. Other studies use a macroeconomic framework to explain the effects of exogenous shocks and government policies on the key macro variables.

The single equation studies have been reviewed by Killick (1984) so that only a summary of their key findings is presented here. Such studies focus mainly on the effects of increases in the prices of imports and of deficit finance on inflation and the balance of payments. According to Killick, increases in the prices of imports - especially the prices of imported inputs - have a significant effect on inflation and worsen the balance of payments. However, money financed deficits are equally important in determining the balance of payments and inflation.

Among the macroeconomic models, Dick *et al* (1983) use a CGE model to examine the short run impact of commodity price instability on domestic prices, employment, and the trade balance. Using a neoclassical optimizing framework, they develop a system of commodity, consumption, investment and factor demand equations for Kenya, Colombia and the Ivory Coast. Their results show that these countries can isolate the effects of the price shocks by pursuing a policy of fixed domestic absorption. However, such a policy requires a high level of foreign exchange reserves which does not exist in many developing countries. They also show that an attempt to keep a balance of trade equilibrium requires a continuous devaluation of the real exchange rate.

A similar model was used by Gupta and Togan (1984) for several developing countries including Kenya. Using a CGE model, they analyzed the effects of liberal and interventionist policy responses on output and income distribution. They concluded that liberal policies tended to minimize GDP losses and thus increased the welfare of farmers. However, such policies reduced the welfare of industrial workers.

Branson (1986) developed a macroeconomic model to evaluate the relative effect of various adjustment policies such as devaluation and a reduction in government spending on investment and output. The model has two sectors (importables and exportables) and incorporates imported inputs, price and wage rigidity. Using parameter values that represent the Kenyan structural features, he showed that a devaluation has more serious contractionary effects on output through its negative effect on investment. He concludes that a reduction in government spending is more favourable than devaluation in an economy like Kenya.

In a more recent study, Bevan, Collier and Gunning (1990) use a CGE model to analyze the fiscal responses to the commodity boom in Kenya. Specifically, they focus on the coffee boom of 1976. Their model incorporates both the neoclassical features of optimization and the key structural features of the Kenyan economy. The structural features include: price and wage inflexibility, imperfect rural financial markets, and a fixed supply of land. Their analysis points out that government spending and foreign borrowing increased following the coffee boom. The net effect on capital formation was negative. Capital formation was reduced by over 65% between 1976 and 1979. Other boom-induced effects were increases in the prices of nontraded goods and real private investment. The increase in private investment was, however, inefficient, largely because of the government controls on private sector spending behaviour.

# 4 The general theoretical framework

## 4.1 Introduction

This chapter develops the general theoretical framework for analysing the structural adjustment processes relevant to the current account in Kenya for the period 1973-1988. Its main objective is to specify a general framework that captures the key elements in the adjustment process. These include: the transmission mechanisms from external shocks to domestic production and spending and their implications for the current account; the response by the key actors in the economy and the manner in which they interact to determine the final outcome. A macroeconomic model (based on the output-absorption approach) of a small open developing economy is first developed. This model is stated and analyzed explicitly in chapter 5.

Early studies in this area focused on the Harberger-Laursen-Metzler effect which analyzed the effects of the terms of trade on saving, investment and the current account (see Harberger 1950; Laursen and Metzler 1950). These studies postulated that a deterioration in the terms of trade reduces real income which in turn reduces saving measured in terms of exportables. Therefore, given the level of investment and no government deficit, a deterioration in the terms of trade would worsen the current account.

Although providing important contributions to open economy macroeconomics, the Harberger-Laursen-Metzler effect relied on a static theory of saving. Recent studies have extended the literature in several directions to examine current account dynamics in an intertemporal framework. Most of these studies analyze the effect of terms of trade changes not only on saving, but also on overall private expenditure (consumption and investment) and hence the current account in an optimizing framework with forward looking agents. The implications of consumption/saving optimization with forward looking behaviour for the current account have been analyzed by: Sachs (1981), Obstfeld (1982), and Svensson and Razin (1983). The role of forward looking investment behaviour in current account determination has been done by Razin (1980), Sachs (1981), Bruno (1982), Svensson (1981), Helpman and Razin (1984), and Gavin (1990), among others. Still other studies have included both saving and expenditures in their analysis. These include: Sachs (1981), Bruno and Sachs (1985) and Conway (1986, 1987). This research has been for developed countries except for Conway's which was undertaken for Turkey, a semi-industrialized country.

This book uses an intertemporal optimization framework is used to analyze the determinants of the current account behaviour in Kenya. Its theoretical specification follows the literature cited above in an attempt to avoid the limitations of other models used to analyze structural adjustments in developing countries (see chapter 2). Most studies on developing countries have relied on partial equilibrium or computable general equilibrium (CGE) models which ignore the interactions among markets and/or make *ad hoc* assumptions regarding the behaviour of the economic agents (Robinson 1989). Also, the models assume structurally invariant parameters which does not satisfy the Lucas critique of economic policy evaluation (Lucas 1976).

The methodology adopted in this book has some similarities with that of Conway (1986, 1987) which combines an intertemporal optimizing macroeconomic model with game theory and estimates it using Turkish data. However, our specification differs from Conway's in several important respects. First, our production structure assumes two production sectors and that structural adjustment is a gradual process. On the latter, it takes time for an economy to adjust fully to changes in external conditions because some factors of production can only be moved between sectors over time. The irreversibility theory of investment emphasizes this with respect to capital.[1]

Our introduction of two production sectors allows the analysis of intersectoral shifts in the economy and the explicit role of relative prices which have an important role in structural adjustment. Also, the effects of both internal and external shocks on the current account can be analyzed through their effects on the relative prices of traded and nontraded goods. Conway's specification assumes a single production sector and therefore abstracts from an explicit treatment of these issues. This book also incorporates the economic and institutional structure of the Kenyan economy into the analysis.

To summarize, the modelling strategy adopted in this book is along the neoclassical approach to structuralism which integrates the neoclassical analysis with the structural theories of growth and development (Bevan, Collier and Gunning 1990). This is in recognition of the emerging view that neoclassical theory has an important role to play in the analysis of growth and development in less developed countries (Lal 1986). Our approach also recognises the structural view that the economic and institutional structure of an economy makes certain patterns of resource allocation more likely than others (Taylor 1983, ch. 1). The key characteristics of the Kenyan economy which will be specified in the theoretical model are:

a) A high degree of openness characterized by dependence on the export of primary commodities and the import of intermediate and capital goods. Further, the economy is very dependent on foreign investment and aid for growth. Therefore, shocks in the international economy are easily transmitted to the Kenyan economy through changes in the terms of trade, in the interest rates, and in the demand for exports.

b) An industrial structure which produces up to 85% of all the final consumer goods required in the country. The industrial sector in Kenya owes its existence to the policy of import substitution which guarantees protection from competing imports through tariffs and other forms of trade controls (Hazlewood 1979). Most of the production is inefficient and the prices of manufactured goods are above international levels. As a result, most of the output is for domestic consumption only. It can, therefore, be assumed that the output of this sector is nontraded.

c) The presence of distortions in the labour market with the wage rate set at a point where the labour market does not clear. Wage formation involves unions, employers, and the government and has indexation. The evidence for Kenya suggests that both institutional and market forces have a role to play in wage determination (Bigsten 1984; Collier and Lal 1986).

d) Agriculture is the dominant sector in terms of the contribution to GDP and employment. Also, the trade balance is heavily influenced by what happens in the agricultural sector because commodity exports form the bulk of the economy's exports. Given the instability of prices and the demand for commodity exports in the world market, the economy is very vulnerable to external shocks. Ikiara (1981) and Hazlewood (1979) have documented this structural dependence on a few export commodities.

e) The distribution of income between agriculture and non-agriculture and/or between wage and non-wage income is important in the determination of growth and development. Resource transfers between agriculture and non-agriculture and their implications for growth have been analyzed by Sharpley

(1981) and the distribution of income in terms of wage and non-wage income by Hazlewood (1979), World Bank (1975) and ILO (1972). Given that agriculture is the largest employer, a redistribution of income towards agriculture has strong implications for the redistribution of income to workers.

## 4.2 The specification of the general model

A stylized structure of the economy producing traded (T) and nontraded goods (N) is considered. The traded goods sector produces primary goods mainly for export but with some domestic consumption. The nontraded goods sector produces final consumer goods mainly for domestic consumption. Both sectors use labour, imported capital and intermediate goods in the production process and are especially dependent on imported intermediate goods. Labour is assumed to be mobile across the sectors but capital is assumed to be specific, especially in the short run, owing to the irreversible nature of many investment projects.

The economy is assumed to lack market power internationally so that the prices of traded goods and the interest rate on borrowing are determined in the world market. The exchange rate is fixed and exchange controls are widely used to ration foreign exchange. Therefore, the domestic prices of capital and traded goods are assumed to equal their foreign levels multiplied by the exchange rate. The nontraded goods price is assumed to be determined by domestic market forces and may be above the international price level. The overall price level is a weighted average of the traded and the nontraded prices. It is assumed that the wage rate does not adjust instantaneously to clear the market and hence unemployment prevails.

To simplify the theoretical exposition, the intertemporal framework is represented by two periods where it is assumed that periods 1 and 2 correspond to the short run and the long run respectively. Perfect foresight of all future variables is assumed. Moreover, the focus will be on the real side of the economy. Monetary variables and an infinite time horizon are introduced in the empirical chapter.

The production and spending behaviour of the economy is as specified in the following subsections.

### 4.2.1 Consumption

The standard intertemporal theory of consumption was developed by Hall (1978) and is based on the permanent income-life cycle models of Friedman (1957), Modigiliani and Brumberg (1954), and Ando and Modigliani (1963).

47

These models recognize that consumers take into account their lifetime resources rather than their current income when making consumption decisions. Hall's contribution was the introduction of the concept of rational expectations in forecasting future income.

The underlying framework of this neoclassical approach to consumption assumes a representative consumer with an intertemporal utility function with its arguments being the consumption in every period. The consumer maximizes this utility function subject to an intertemporal budget constraint such that the present (discounted) value of his expenditure cannot exceed the present (discounted) value of his wealth. Perfect capital markets are assumed so that borrowing and lending are possible at the prevailing interest rate.

As noted earlier, the theoretical analysis is being simplified by assuming perfect foresight and a two period framework. The consumer is taken to maximize:

$$U = U(C^T_1, C^N_1, C^T_2, C^N_2) = u(C^T_1, C^N_1) + \Psi u(C^T_2, C^N_2) \qquad (4.1)$$

subject to:

$$P^T_1.C^T_1 + P^N_1.C^N_1 + \Phi(P^T_2.C^T_2 + P^N_2.C^N_2) \leq \omega \qquad (4.2)$$

where:

| | |
|---|---|
| $U(.)$ | intertemporal utility function |
| $u(.)$ | period utility function |
| $C^j$ | consumption of the jth good, $j = N,T$ |
| $P^j$ | price of jth good, $j = N,T$ |
| $\omega$ | total wealth |
| $\Psi$ | subjective discount factor = $(1+\text{rate of time preference})^{-1}$ |
| $\Phi$ | market discount factor = $(1+\text{rate of interest})^{-1}$ |

The superscripts T and N represent traded and nontraded goods and subscripts 1 and 2 represent periods 1 and 2 respectively. The utility functions $U(.)$ and $u(.)$ assumed to be strictly concave, and monotonic. The intertemporal utility function $U(.)$ is specified as separable in the period utility functions and the period utility functions $u(.)$ have been assumed to be identical and homothetic.

The consumer's problem can be summarized as the minimization of expenditure E to attain a given level of utility $\underline{U}$. That is:

Minimize $E(P^T_1, P^N_1, P^T_2, P^N_2, \Phi, \Psi, \underline{U})$

$$= \text{Min.} \ \{P^T_1.C^T_1 + P^N_1.C^N_1 + \Phi(P^T_2.C^T_2 + P^N_2.C^N_2)\} \quad (4.3)$$

subject to:

$$u(C^T_1, C^N_1) + \Psi u(C^T_2, C^N_2) \geq \underline{U} \quad (4.4)$$

The expenditure function E(.) is assumed to have all the desired duality properties.[2] Applying Shephard's Lemma, the compensated demand functions for both goods are:

$$C^T_1 = C^T_1(P^T_1, P^N_1, P^T_2, P^N_2, \Phi, \Psi, \underline{U}) \quad (4.5)$$

$$C^N_1 = C^N_1(P^T_1, P^N_1, P^T_2, P^N_2, \Phi, \Psi, \underline{U}) \quad (4.6)$$

$$C^T_2 = C^T_2(P^T_1, P^N_1, P^T_2, P^N_2, \Phi, \Psi, \underline{U}) \quad (4.7)$$

$$C^N_2 = C^N_2(P^T_1, P^N_1, P^T_2, P^N_2, \Phi, \Psi, \underline{U}) \quad (4.8)$$

The partial derivative of each of these demand functions with respect to its own price in each period is taken to be negative - that is, the own price effect is assumed to be negative. The two goods are assumed to be net substitutes and, as demonstrated by Edwards (1989), the intratemporal cross price effects are positive. The assumption of time separable utility function implies that expenditures in periods 1 and 2 are substitutes (Edwards 1989, p. 345). Consequently, all the intertemporal cross price effects are negative.

In the Kenyan context, exports are the only traded good produced in the economy. Imports are determined residually as the difference between total consumption expenditures and expenditures on domestically produced goods. This is because imports of final consumer goods are only allowed when a domestic substitute is unavailable. Hence, there is no substitution between imported and domestic consumer goods. This implies that the utility function can be assumed to be weakly separable between imported and domestic consumer goods. The intertemporal framework developed by Hall (1978) is general and can be applied to any economy to test the permanent income-rational expectations hypothesis. However, as Deaton (1990) has argued, the features of most developing countries may not deliver the standard result that consumption is proportional to permanent income, as postulated for developed countries. This hypothesis is examined below and its implications for the

Kenyan situation are discussed.

Deaton notes that the standard household in developing countries tends to be larger than in developed countries and has a tendency to have a stationary demographic structure. Older people are replaced by the young as they die and each person moves up the demographic ladder. Also, resources are shared within the family and ownership is transferred from generation to generation. Parents 'invest' in the young by subsidizing their consumption as they mature in exchange for support in old age.

For such a household, there is no need for retirement or life cycle saving since the household provides insurance against old age. Moreover, the stationary demographic structure and the intergenerational transfers suggest that the average household tends to live longer than the average individual. This supports the idea of a dynasty of consumers. The life cycle model, with its assumption of a finite time horizon, is inconsistent with this notion of a dynasty of consumers. However, the latter is consistent with Friedman's permanent income hypothesis which is not bound by a finite time horizon.

Most households in the developing countries derive their income from agriculture, either directly or indirectly. Given the uncertainty associated with agricultural incomes, saving provides a buffer between the uncertain and unpredictable income, and a low level of consumption. Saving thus tends to be 'high-frequency' intergenerational smoothing of consumption and not life-cycle hump or intragenerational saving (Deaton 1989, p. 65). Related to this is the unavailability of credit when income is less than the desired permanent level of consumption. The available evidence shows that most households in developing countries tend to be liquidity constrained (Gersovitz 1989).

Kenya shares the above characteristics with other developing countries. The idea of a dynasty of consumers supports the application of the rational expectations-permanent income hypothesis which is consistent with the assumption that the consumer lives for ever (Abel 1990). However, the presence of liquidity constrained consumers violates one of the crucial assumptions of this hypothesis. Following current research in the field, this book incorporates the effects of liquidity constraints.

### 4.2.2 Production

Production of traded and nontraded goods is carried out according to the following production functions which are assumed to be strictly quasi-concave, twice differentiable, homothetic and with positive first order derivatives.

$$Y^T_t = F^T(K^T_t, N^T_t, E^T_t) \tag{4.9}$$

$$Y^N_t = F^N(K^N_t, N^N_t, E^N_t) \tag{4.9}$$

where:

| | |
|---|---|
| Y | output |
| F(.) | production function |
| K | capital |
| N | labour |
| E | imported inputs |

The subscript t represents periods 1 and 2 and the superscripts specify the relevant goods sector.

Part of the capital equipment and intermediate inputs are produced domestically but in negligible amounts. The domestic components are therefore assumed away. As noted earlier, labour is assumed to be mobile across sectors and capital is sector specific which can be explained by the irreversibility theory of investment (Pindyck 1989).

The assumption that the price of traded goods is determined internationally is consistent with the Kenyan situation because traded goods are dominated by primary exports like coffee and tea whose prices are determined by international market forces. Regarding nontraded goods, there is government intervention in the pricing of some of the essential goods. However, the assumption that pricing is mainly driven by domestic market forces is still valid because there has been a steady decline over the years in the number of controlled items and also because price reviews on controlled items are mainly influenced by market forces (Mukui 1978).

The labour market is assumed to have distortions which inhibit full wage flexibility and the level of real wages is such that there is excess supply of labour in both periods. Employment is thus determined by demand. Theoretically, wage rigidities can be explained by the dual economy theories of growth associated with Lewis (1954) and Ranis and Fei (1961). Also, neoclassical theories which incorporate uncertainty, risk and moral hazard in the labour market can explain why wages tend to be rigid (Collier and Lal 1986).

In the Kenyan case, the available evidence suggests that wage setting is influenced by both institutional and market forces (Bigsten 1984; Collier and Lal 1986). The government sets wage guidelines based on trends in growth and inflation. Workers and employers then follow these guidelines during the bargaining process. Market forces play a role in the way these wage guidelines are set and the extent to which the government enforces them.

The intertemporal production decisions are assumed to be governed by the maximization of discounted profits subject to the technological constraints in both sectors and for the given factor and product prices. In the assumed two period framework, there is only one investment decision. This follows from the assumption that the capital stock in period 1 is already installed and producers choose optimal investment in period 1 to attain the desired capital stock in period 2.

Bruno and Sachs (1985) have shown that the intertemporal maximization of profits as explained above produces two sets of optimality conditions. One set is the standard first order conditions for profit maximization for each period separately. The second is an intertemporal requirement which describes optimal investment behaviour in period one or the desired capital stock in period two.

From the above observations, the producers' behaviour is derived from the maximization of their profits. That is, they maximize:

$$\pi^j_1(P^j_1, W_1, P^E_1, K^j_1) = P^j_1 . Y^j_1 - W_1 N^j_1 - P^E_1 E^j_1 \qquad (4.11)$$

$$\pi^j_2(P^j_2, W_2, P^E_2, P^K_2) = P^j_2 . Y^j_2 - W_2 N^j_2$$

$$- P^E_2 E^j_2 - P^K_2 . K^j_2 \qquad (4.12)$$

where:

| | |
|---|---|
| $\pi$ | profit |
| W | nominal wage rate |
| $P^E$ | price of imported inputs |

The superscript j represents the two sectors (i.e., $j = T,N$) and the subscripts represent periods 1 and 2. All the other variables are as defined earlier. The technological constraints are as in equations (4.9) and (4.10) above. The capital stock in period one is assumed to be already installed and producers choose optimal investment to attain the desired capital stock in period 2. Substituting the technological constraints in the respective profit functions in equations (4.11) and (4.12), and using Hotteling's Lemma, the following supply and demand functions are obtained:

$$Y^j_1 = \partial \pi^j_1 / \partial P^j_1 = Y^j_1(P^j_1, W_1, P^E_1, K^j_1) \qquad (4.13)$$

$$Y^j_2 = \partial \pi^j_2 / \partial P^j_2 = Y^j_2(P^j_2, W_2, P^E_2, P^K_2) \qquad (4.14)$$

$$N^j_1 = \partial \pi^j_1 / \partial W^j_1 = N^j_1(P^j_1, W_1, P^E_1, K^j_1) \qquad (4.15)$$

$$E^j_1 = \partial \pi^j_1 / \partial P^j_1 = E^j_1(P^j_1, W_1, P^E_1, K^j_1) \qquad (4.16)$$

$$N^j_2 = \partial \pi^j_2 / \partial W^j_2 = N^j_2(P^j_2, W_2, P^E_2, P^K_2) \qquad (4.17)$$

$$E^j_2 = \partial \pi^j_2 / \partial P^j_2 = E^j_2(P^j_2, W_2, P^E_2, P^K_2) \qquad (4.18)$$

The supply and demand functions for period 1 are derived from a restricted profit function because the capital stock in period 1 is given. Therefore, the capital stock of period 1 enters the functions as an independent variable.

The level of investment is defined as the difference between the optimal capital stock in period 2 and the given stock in period 1. The optimal capital stock and hence the level of investment can be derived from the neoclassical theory of investment as developed by Jorgenson (1967) and Hall and Jorgenson (1967). This approach uses profit or cost functions to derive the optimal capital stock. Using the profit functions of equations (4.11) and (4.12), the optimal capital stock can be expressed as a function of the price of output, the wage rate, the price of imported inputs, and the rental rate of capital which in turn depends on the price of capital and the interest rate. Conway (1987) and Marrion and Svenson (1984) have used a similar approach.

An alternative approach to the above neoclassical theory is Tobin's q theory of investment (Tobin 1969). This theory focuses on the variable q which is the ratio of the market value of the existing capital stock to its replacement cost as the main determinant of investment. It specifies that under certain conditions such perfect capital markets and absence of adjustment costs, investment will be undertaken up to that point where Tobin's q is equal to 1. However, the critical ratio will differ from 1 in the presence of costs associated with delivery lags and increasing marginal costs of investment. Abel (1982) and Hayashi (1982) have shown that if the costs of adjustment are convex, the neoclassical theory and Tobin's q theory lead to the same result.

The optimal capital stock in period 2 for both the sectors is derived from the requirement that the present value of the marginal productivity of capital at the exogenously given interest rate should be equal to the purchase price of capital in period 1. This approach has been used in a number of studies including Conway (1987), Marion and Svenson (1982) and Razin (1980). Mathematically, this can be expressed as:

$$\partial \pi^j / \partial K^j = K^j_2(P^j_2, W_2, P^E_2)/i^*_2 = P^K_1 \qquad (4.19)$$

where $i^*_t$ is the world interest rate in period t. In equilibrium, investment will be undertaken up to the point where the rates of return in both the sectors are equalized. Given our assumption that real investment augments capital with a lag of one period, the capital stock in the second period can be expressed as follows:

$$K^j_2 = K^j_1 + I^j_1 \qquad (4.20)$$

where $I^j$ is investment in sector j. I is defined a total investment and is the sum of investment in both sectors, with $I = I^N + I^T$.

Given the initial capital stock $K^j_1$ in period 1, its rate of depreciation $\delta$ and the optimal capital stock $K^j_2$ as determined by equation (4.19) for period 2, investment in period 1 is determined by:

$$I^j_1 = K^j_2(P^j_2, W_1, P^E_2, P^K_1, i^*_2) - (1 - \delta) K^j_1 \qquad (4.21)$$

In the case of a developing country such as Kenya, investment would be subject to a number of constraints which do not appear in the theories cited above. A more relevant theory is the disequilibrium approach which identifies two steps in the investment decision making process (Malinvaud 1982). The first one is a decision to increase productive capacity and the second one is the decision to determine the factor intensity of the investment. The former depends on demand conditions (sales) which determine the level of capacity utilization. Therefore, the sales constraints would enter as an additional determinant of investment. The factor intensity of investment depends on relative factor prices.

The other constraints which tend to affect investment in the developing countries include foreign exchange and credit availability.[3] In the Kenyan case, the evidence suggests that foreign exchange constraints are a significant factor in formulating investment decisions. Also, the level of demand is the main determinant of capacity utilization (Coughlin and Ikiara 1988). These other determinants of investment will be tested in the Kenyan case in the empirical part of this book.

## 4.3 Private sector equilibrium

Equilibrium is attained when both production and consumption decisions are optimal. Assuming a competitive framework, this condition is attained at the point where the marginal rate of transformation between the two goods is equal to their marginal rate of substitution in consumption; which is also equal to the ratio of their respective prices. Although a competitive framework may not conform to the Kenyan situation, there are useful inferences which can be drawn from such an assumption.

It is useful to work with the duals of the production and utility functions because they focus on the variables of our immediate interest. Production and utility functions focus on quantities while their duals - that is cost and expenditure functions - focus on prices, keeping quantities in the background.[4] Our analysis of structural adjustment focuses on changes in relative prices and their impact on resource reallocation. It is, therefore, more convenient for us to proceed with the cost and expenditure functions.

We assume that there are no borrowing and/or lending constraints, and that the rate of interest is given. Under such conditions, the intertemporal allocation of consumption is independent of the optimal choice of factor inputs. Consequently, the production and consumption decisions can be analyzed separately.[5]

The duality between the production and cost functions implies that the optimal factor demands can be analyzed in terms of the unit cost function. The unit cost function indicates the minimum cost of producing one unit of output at given factor prices. For the production function assumed here, the unit cost function can be represented by:

$$C^j_1 = C^j_1(W_1, P^E_1, K^j_1) \tag{4.22}$$

$$C^j_2 = C^j_2(W_2, P^E_2, K^j_2) \tag{4.23}$$

These two unit cost functions correspond to the restricted and the unrestricted profit functions in equations (4.11) and (4.12). For a profit maximizing firm, equilibrium is attained at that point where price equals marginal cost. This is equivalent to the following conditions:

$$P^j_1 = C^j_1(W_1, P^E_1, K^j_1) \tag{4.24}$$

$$P^j_2 = C^j_2(W_2, P^E_2, P^K_2) \tag{4.25}$$

These equilibrium conditions trace isoprice lines for the two commodities (j = T, N). These lines represent combinations of the wage rate and the price of capital that are consistent with profit maximization.

Figure 1 shows the isoprice curves corresponding to equations (4.18) and (4.19). It is based on the work of Mussa (1979) and Woodland (1982).

In figure 4.1, $P^N$ and $P^T$ are the isoprofit curves for the nontraded and the traded goods respectively and are drawn for a given price ($P^E$) of imported inputs.[6] The isoprofit curves are convex to the origin and their curvatures represent the elasticities of substitution in the respective sectors. The convexity of the isoprice curves implies that the ratio of the wage rate to the price of capital is positively related to the capital-labour ratio. This rules out reswitching of techniques. Also the two curves must intersect only once to avoid factor intensity reversals. The point of intersection, A, embodies the equilibrium wage rate and the price of capital consistent with profit maximization. Also, point A represents optimal factor demands. The capital-labour ratios for both sectors can be obtained from the slopes of lines BAC and DAE.

Figure 4.1 shows the case where the capital-labour ratio for the nontraded sector is higher than the one for the traded goods sector. Increasing $P^T$ or $P^N$ shifts the respective isoprice curve to the right, while an increase in $P^E$ shifts them inwards. The impact of external shocks can be analyzed by considering the effects of changes in $P^T$, $P^N$, and $P^E$.

The intertemporal allocation of consumption is shown in Figure 4.2 for the case of nontraded goods using a modified Fisher diagram as in Svensson (1981). A consumption possibilities frontier (C.P.F.) is drawn representing the combinations of consumption in periods 1 and 2 in the absence of borrowing and lending. This frontier is defined by the optimal combinations of the consumption of the nontraded goods for periods 1 and 2. In the absence of credit, the equilibrium is at point E where the highest social indifference curve is tangent to the C.P.F. The social indifference curves are derived from the expenditure function in equation (4.3) above. Borrowing at the world interest rate i* allows the country to be on the straight line through G. This line has a slope equal to $[-P^N_2/P^N_1 (1+r^*)]$ or, at constant prices, equal to $[-1/(1+r^*)]$. Borrowing at the world interest rate r* allows the country to move to G and thereby increase its social welfare. Figure 4.2 is drawn for the case where moving from E to G only increases consumption in period 1. If G, the point of tangency of the highest attainable indifference curve to the opportunity locus with external borrowing, was to the right of E but above E, consumption in both periods would increase. In this case, both consumption and investment in period 1 will increase, since investment in period 1 produces deferred consumption in period 2.

**Figure 4.1**

**Equilibrium in production**

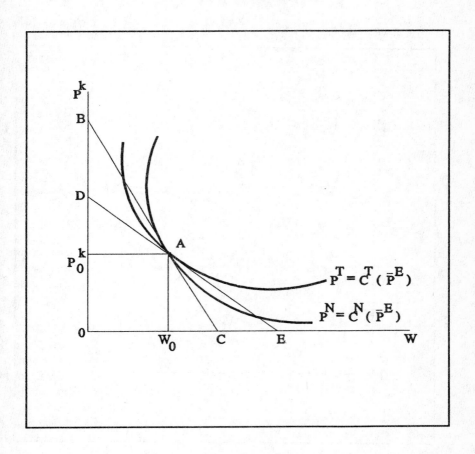

**Figure 4.2**

**Private intertemporal consumption decisions**

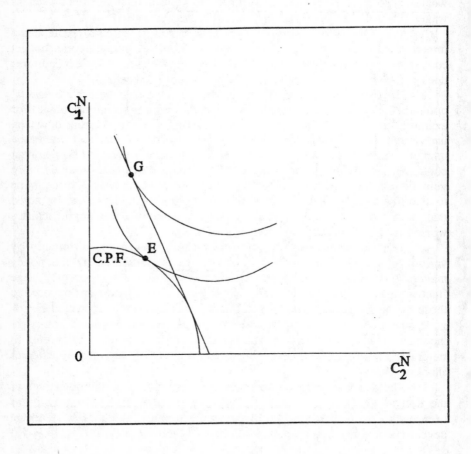

## 4.4 The behaviour of the government

Our model assumes that the government maximizes social welfare either directly or indirectly using the policy instruments at its disposal. Social welfare can be maximized by undertaking investment expenditures to increase growth and/or redistribute income. The policy instruments available include government expenditures and the taxation of exports, imports, income and/or wealth. The government can also decide to control relative prices such as wages, the real exchange rate and domestic interest rates.

The government is assumed to have access to foreign credit at the internationally determined interest rate. It faces an intertemporal budget constraint specifying that the present (discounted) value of its expenditures does not exceed the present (discounted) value of its receipts.

The rationale for the government's actions is that the private agents' optimal behaviour does not always coincide with what is socially optimal. For example, producers may respond to an external shock by cutting down on investment, an action which results in reduced growth and increased unemployment. To maintain growth and employment targets, the government could step in to increase investment. Also, some social groups may be more vulnerable to external shocks than others and the government could intervene to stabilize their income and/or expenditures. It should, however, be noted that, under certain conditions, the government intervention might actually worsen the problems instead of alleviating them.

The various economic groups which may be affected differently by various types of the external shocks need to be identified by the policy makers. For example, the producers of traded goods are exposed to large fluctuations in commodity prices which destabilize their income as opposed to those of the firms in the nontraded sector which is heavily protected by the government. A similar distinction can be made between wage and non-wage incomes. Under such circumstances, the government may intervene to minimize the loss of welfare of those groups adversely affected by external shocks.

The above description approximates very closely to the objectives of the Kenyan government since independence. Redistribution with growth has been one of the main objectives of government policy, as indicated in all the development plans (see Republic of Kenya, 1966-70, 1971-1974, 1974-78, 1978-1982, 1983-87). Further, the traded goods sector in Kenya experiences large fluctuations in income owing to its dependence on commodity exports. The workers' real incomes are affected by both external and domestic forces.

We assume that the Kenyan government's optimization behaviour can be summarized as a maximization of the following quadratic loss function:[7]

$$\Omega = -(\Omega_1 - \Omega^*_1)^2 - \rho(\Omega_2 - \Omega^*_2)^2 \qquad (4.26)$$

where:

$$\Omega_1 = N.(W_1/P_1) + C^c_1$$

$$\Omega_2 = N.(W_2/P_2) + C^c_2$$

and:

| | |
|---|---|
| $\Omega_1$ | consumption in period 1 |
| $\Omega_2$ | consumption in period 2 |
| W | nominal wage |
| P | overall price level |
| $\rho$ | discount factor |
| $C^c$ | capitalist consumption (i.e. consumption from nonwage income) |

We have assumed that workers consume all their income.

The loss function (4.26) specifies that the government is concerned with the distribution of consumption between wage and non-wage income earners. It is also concerned with the distribution of consumption between the current period and the future. This is captured through the weights attached to $\Omega_1$ and $\Omega_2$. As noted earlier, it is also possible to incorporate other distributional considerations by looking at the distribution of income between the traded and nontraded sectors. However, we have concentrated on the distinction between wage and nonwage income, mainly because the available income distribution data are primarily in terms of the functional distribution of income. In any case, most structuralist studies use this distinction in analysing income distribution.[8]

The loss function (4.26) can be interpreted as a social welfare function which embodies both intra- and inter-temporal considerations. This social welfare function depends on private sector behaviour, governmental policies and the exogenous variables of the system. Private sector behaviour has been discussed in sections 4.2 and 4.3 above. The following discusses the relevance of governmental policies.

We consider an exchange rate policy as an illustration of government policy actions. Given the theoretical structure of the model, the exchange rate policy is only useful in period 1 because in period 2 there is a complete pass through of the devaluation to domestic prices. The government's use of exchange policy may be in response to unfavourable external conditions or domestic forces which lead to an over-valued real exchange rate. The reason for devaluation may, therefore, be to improve competitiveness and enhance growth. However, the government is well aware of the negative effects of devaluation on production: private investors would cut back on investment and employment would decline after a devaluation. Increases in the prices of imports have an equivalent effect to devaluation and will not be dealt with in detail.

Figure 4.3 shows how the government chooses the optimal combinations of the real exchange rate $R_1$, and private investment $I^P$, to maximize social welfare. This figure uses the concept of isowelfare curves (or social ovals) to represent combinations of $R_1$ and $I^P$ that lead to the same level of welfare given the optimal behaviour of the private and public sectors. The isowelfare curves are derived by totally differentiating the loss function with respect to $R_1$ and $I^P$, given a particular level of welfare. Suppressing all the other variables, the social welfare function takes the following form:

$$\Omega = \Omega(R_1, I^P) \tag{4.27}$$

Differentiating totally with respect to the two variables:

$$(\partial\Omega/\partial R_1 | I^P).dR_1 + (\partial\Omega/\partial I^P | R_1).dI^P = 0 \tag{4.28}$$

In figure 4.3, the tradeoffs between $I^P$ and $R_1$ are indicated by lines $G_1$ and $G_2$ for periods 1 and 2 respectively. They are derived from equation (4.27) by setting the two partial derivatives in equation (4.28) equal to zero, as in:

$$(\partial\Omega/\partial R_1 | I^P) = 0 \quad \text{and} \quad (\partial\Omega/\partial I^P | R_1) = 0 \tag{4.29}$$

The intertemporal optimal combination of $R_1$ and $I^P$ is attained at the intersection of $G_1$ and $G_2$ which also gives the point of maximum welfare. In the event that the highest welfare point is not attainable, the government will be obliged to choose that combination of $R_1$ and $I^P$ that is tangent to the highest attainable social oval. The government's choice of $R_1$ is not independent of the behaviour of the private sector. Therefore, it has to take into account the reaction of the private sector when formulating its exchange rate policy. This interaction can be modeled as a game between the government and the private sector and is discussed in the section below.

## 4.5 The interaction between the private sector and the government

The introduction of game theory in the determination of overall equilibrium is justified when an outcome is a function not only of the optimal behaviour of the two agents but also of their interaction. Recent studies in macroeconomics recognize this interdependence between the government and the private sector and analyze it as a game between the two actors.[9] The theoretical aspects of game theory are dealt with here only in so far as they relate to the interaction between the private sector and the government.

The interaction between the government and the private sector is assumed to be a non-cooperative game in the sense that collusion between them through binding agreements is not possible or does not exist. The payoffs are measured in terms of private sector utility and social welfare. The game is played in both periods and each of the choices is constrained to be non-negative. Perfect foresight is being assumed so that each player knows the optimal responses of the other.

The outcomes are dependent on how the game is played and the timing structures involved. Two types of games are assumed. In one, both players choose their strategies concurrently and without the knowledge of each other's strategy. In the second one, a Stackleberg game is assumed with the government as the leader. The government's choice of $R_1$ and $I^p$ in the previous section is used to derive the theoretical outcomes of the two games.

The reaction functions of both the private sector and the government are indicated by the first order conditions of equations (4.13) to (4.18); and the derivative of the investment function (equation (4.21)) with respect to $R_1$. Devaluation affects investment through its effect on the price of imported inputs. The derivative is negative indicating that a devaluation reduces profitability and reduces investment through changes in the price of imported inputs. The corresponding reaction function for the government is obtained by differentiating the objective function with respect to $R_1$ for a given $I^p$.

A devaluation has an effect on all of the first order conditions (4.13) to (4.18). To obtain the optimal response functions of both the private sector and the government, it is necessary to substitute these optimal conditions into the private sector investment reaction function (i.e., the derivative of equation (4.21) with respect to $R_1$) and the government's reaction function.

The reaction functions are represented by pp and $G_t$ in figure 4.4. $G_t$ is the government's reaction function in period t. pp is below $G_2$ because the government prefers a higher period 2 capital stock at each $R_1$ since this provides more employment and income for workers. The intersection of $G_1$ and pp at A provides the concurrent outcome. B is the Stackleberg outcome.

To get to B, the government chooses an $R_1$ along pp which gives the highest social welfare. This is consistent with private sector optimal response and it yields the highest welfare. Some of the parameters which determine the position of the curves $G_1$, $G_2$ and pp have useful economic interpretation. For instance, a high rate of social time preference implies that the social ovals become narrower around $G_1$. In the extreme case, both outcomes (Stackleberg and the concurrent) coincide. Also the gap between pp and $G_2$ depends on the elasticity of substitution between labour and capital. A high elasticity means a narrower gap and in the case of infinite elasticity, the two outcomes coincide.

In figure 4.4, the scenario drawn is one where the Stackleberg solution leads to a higher social welfare than the concurrent outcome. Therefore, the government would be expected to prefer it. In this case, the government would be better off if it announced its strategy and then let the private sector respond by incorporating the government strategy in its optimization.

**Figure 4.3**

**The government's optimal choices**

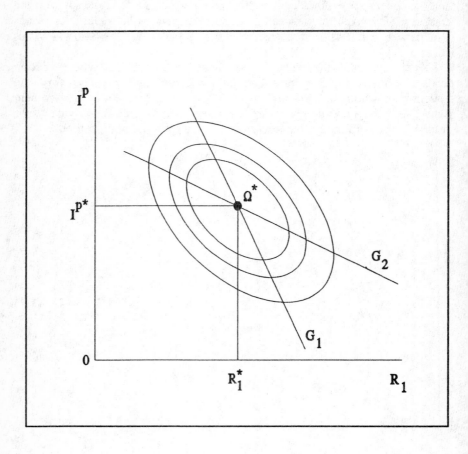

## Figure 4.4

## Equilibrium governmental and private sector choices

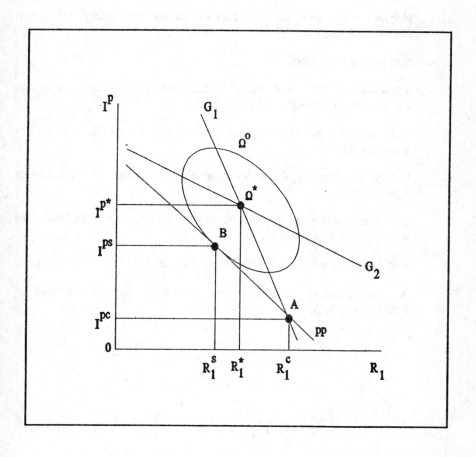

## NOTES

1. For a concise review of the theories of investment, see Solimano (1989).

2. For an application of duality theory to consumer behaviour, see Varian (1984) and Krepps (1990).

3. See Solimano (1989).

4. Woodland (1982) and Sgro (1986) provide a fairly complete application of duality theory in international trade.

5. This reasoning has been used by Conway (1987) and Gavin (1990) in a similar situation.

6. In figures 4.1 to 4.4, the underlining of a symbol has been replaced by a bar over it.

7. This function is a fairly standard form of a loss function and was also used by Conway (1987).

8. For example, see Taylor (1983) and Kalecki (1971).

9. A comprehensive theoretical introduction to this is available in Friedman (1986).

# 5 The theoretical model and econometric estimation

## 5.1 Introduction

The general framework in chapter 4 provides a basis for the model presented in this chapter to explain the structural adjustment to external shocks and its implications for the current account in Kenya. The chapter then estimates the model using Kenyan data for the period 1964-1988. The results are used to analyze the behaviour of the current account. The estimating equations are derived from the theoretical model but are modified to include other possible explanatory variables. These other explanatory variables are drawn from other competing hypotheses about the behavioral equations of the system. This approach enables us to nest our model in a wider framework and to judge how well our model performs relative to other hypotheses.

The empirical results enable us to answer several other questions which were raised in chapters 3 and 4. These are:

i. Is an intertemporal optimizing framework a valid representation of the Kenyan economy?

ii. Is the rational expectations hypothesis valid for a developing economy like Kenya?

iii. To what extent are institutional and structural features important in explaining economic behaviour in Kenya?

iv. How responsive is private agents' behaviour to government policy?

v.    How responsive are private sector expenditure and production behaviour to external shocks?

Chapter 3 had noted two competing explanations for the persistence of current account deficits in developing countries. The structuralist explanation is based on the hypothesis that the low elasticities of substitution in production and expenditure in these countries inhibit the necessary adjustments to correct a deficit following an external shock. The neoclassical explanation rejects the structuralist view and argues that the economy is flexible enough to accommodate external shocks. However, the government's policy responses to the shocks influence private sector behaviour in the 'wrong' direction and thus worsen the current account. The estimated model nests both these possibilities.

To facilitate empirical analysis, several adjustments to the theoretical framework are necessary. First, the two period framework is extended to a multiperiod framework and the assumption of perfect foresight is replaced by the rational expectations assumption. This is in line with recent developments in the literature. Although the validity of the rational expectations assumption in developing countries has been questioned in some parts of the literature, we would like to test for it in our context.

Second, only a one sector model is adopted in this chapter. Despite the advantages of the two sector model set out in chapter 4, data limitations do not allow its estimation. The data problems associated with the classification of the economy into traded and nontraded goods sectors have been well documented in Goldstein *et al* (1980). Despite these limitations, the explanatory variables derived from the two sector framework in chapter 4 will be incorporated in the empirical analysis. Also, published data on gross output (Q) are not available for Kenya. It will be estimated by adding domestic value added (Y) at factor cost to imported inputs (E).

The rest of the chapter is organized as follows: section 2 discusses some econometric issues that have implications for the inferences drawn from the estimated equations. Sections 3 to 5 report parameter estimates for private production, consumption and investment equations. Section 6 provides estimates of government behavioral equations. The interaction between the government and the private sector is reported in section 7.

## 5.2 Econometric issues

The econometric issues discussed in this section apply to all the estimated equations of the model. Any econometric problems associated with a specific equation are discussed in the relevant section. In particular, we discuss the following problems which have serious implications for the validity of the inferences drawn from time series data: stationarity of time series data; departures from the assumption of normality of error terms; serial correlation and the diagnostic tests associated with the econometric problems.

In econometric modelling, the standard inference procedures are heavily dependent on the assumption that the relevant time series are stationary. Violation of this assumption invalidates the inferences drawn from the estimated parameters (Dolado *et al* 1990). Although an important issue, it was not until recently that stationarity of time series data was given adequate attention in empirical work. Most studies on developing countries ignored the problems associated with the nonstationarity of time series mainly because the early testing procedures relied on large data samples which are not usually available for these countries. Recently, Mackinon (1990) developed test statistics based on the Dickey and Fuller (1979) test for any sample size.

To determine whether our time series are stationary, we ran an Augmented Dickey-Fuller (ADF) test for a unit root using Micro TSP version 7.0. This involves the regression of the first difference of each variable against its lagged value, and lagged difference terms. An optional constant term and a trend variable can be specified in the regression. The critical values developed by Mackinon are then used to determine the significance of the coefficients. If the coefficient of the lagged variable is significantly different from 0, the null hypothesis implying the existence of a unit root is rejected. The results are reported in Appendix II to this chapter. The results show that when our series are in logarithmic form, the evidence for nonstationarity in our series is very weak. The regressions can, therefore, be undertaken in logarithmic form.

Most of the statistical inferences also depend on whether the error terms of the regression are normally distributed. These include the F and the students t statistics. We use the Jarque-Berra (JB) statistic to test for this assumption in our study. This statistic is distributed as a $\chi^2$ with 2 degrees of freedom. This implies that the critical value at the 5% level of significance is 5.99. Under the null, the hypothesis of normality in the error terms is rejected if the computed statistic is less than the critical value.

We also provide test statistics for autocorrelation. In the absence of the lagged dependent variable, the Durbin-Watson (DW) statistic is adequate for testing the existence of first order serial correlation. The DW will be used in conjunction with the Lagrange Multiplier (LM) test which is applicable to any form of autocorrelation and is independent of the influence of lagged dependent variables. The LM statistic is also distributed as a $\chi^2$ with degrees of freedom equal to the number of lagged error terms in the regression (i.e., the form of autocorrelation).

In addition, we report the ARCH statistic which tests for the existence of autoregressive conditional heteroscedasticity. As noted by Engle (1982), this type of heteroscedasticity is common in time series data. The ARCH statistic is distributed as a $\chi^2$, as is the LM test. It should however be noted that the JB, LM and the ARCH statistics are not exact. Their distributions are known for large sample sizes and care should be taken in using them when the sample size is small. A concise discussion of these diagnostic tests is provided in Spanos (1989).

## 5.3 Private production

The general specification of our model in chapter 4 assumed that the production of gross output Q is separable in domestic value added Y and imported inputs E. Domestic value added Y was assumed to be a function of capital K and labour N. This two level production structure allows us to capture the degree of substitutability between domestic and imported inputs which is one of the main structural features emphasized in this book.

For empirical purposes, we assume that domestic value added is a Cobb-Douglas function of capital and labour. A constant elasticity of substitution (CES) is assumed between domestic value added and imported inputs. The two production functions are:

$$Y = K^\alpha .N^{(1-\alpha)} \tag{5.1}$$

$$Q = [d.Y^\rho + (1-d).E^\rho]^{1/\rho} \tag{5.2}$$

The variables are as defined before and d, $\rho$ and $\alpha$ are parameters. A similar specification was used by Branson (1986) to analyze the contractionary effects of devaluation in Kenya. It has also been used in other studies including Bruno and Sachs (1985); and Martson and Turnovsky (1983).

The specification above allows the elasticity of substitution between capital and labour to differ from the elasticity of substitution between domestic value added and imported inputs. The Cobb-Douglas specification implies that the elasticity of substitution between capital and labour is equal to unity. A number of empirical studies using both cross section and time series data support this for the Kenyan case. The studies are reviewed in Maitha and Manundu (1981).

The institutional and structural features assumed in chapter 4 imply that the elasticity of substitution between domestic value added and imported inputs in Kenya is very low. This is due to the heavy reliance on imported inputs in the production process. The specification of a CES function requires this elasticity to be constant but allows it to be less than unity.

The elasticity of substitution between imported inputs and domestic value added has not been empirically tested in Kenya. We test the hypothesis that it is statistically different from zero. We use the following equation implied by the first order profit maximization conditions and developed by Arrow, Chenery, Minhas and Solow (1961):

$$\log (Q/E) = b + \{1/(1-\rho)\} \log (P^E/P) \tag{5.3}$$

where:

| | |
|---|---|
| $P^E$ | price of imported inputs |
| $P$ | GDP deflator |

It can be shown that the elasticity of substitution ($\sigma$) is equal to $1/(1-\rho)$ for the CES function above. Equation (5.3) was estimated using the ordinary least squares method. The estimated elasticity of substitution was 0.41 and was statistically significant at the five percent level. This result supports the structural features assumed in chapter 4. Consequently, exogenous shocks and structural adjustment policies that increase the price of imported inputs have serious contractionary effects, thus confirming Taylor's (1983) hypothesis.

The first order maximization conditions of chapter 4 allow us to derive the demand functions for labour and imported inputs by equating their marginal products with their respective real factor prices. In the case of the separable CES function specified above, the demand functions for imported inputs and labour are:

$$E_t = (1-d)^\sigma (P^E/P)_t^{-\sigma} Q_t \tag{5.4}$$

$$N_t = (W_t/P_t)^\beta K_t^{\beta'} Q_t^{\beta''} \tag{5.5}$$

where:

$$\beta = \sigma/[\alpha(1-\sigma) - \sigma)]$$

$$\beta' = \alpha_1(1-\sigma) - \sigma$$

$$\beta'' = [-(1-\alpha)(1-\sigma)]/[\alpha(1-\sigma) - \sigma]$$

71

$$\sigma = 1/(1-\rho)$$

The actual derivations of equations (5.3), (5.4) and (5.5) are shown in Appendix I of this chapter.

Equations (5.1), (5.2), (5.4), and (5.5) represent the production structure of the economy. The capital stock is assumed to be given and therefore is an explanatory variable. The wage rate is assumed to be determined by government policy and, given the small country assumption, the price of imported inputs is exogenously determined. The two factor prices are therefore exogenous and are independent variables.

Equations (5.1), (5.2), (5.4) and (5.5) form a set of simultaneous equations and should be estimated by an instrumental variables technique to avoid the simultaneous equations bias. To simplify estimation, we assume that the functions are observed with a multiplicative error and that technological progress is Hicks-neutral. The assumption that technological progress is Hicks-neutral is convenient for estimation purposes although it may not conform to the experience of some developing countries.

The set of equations (5.1), (5.4) and (5.5) was estimated using the two stage least squares technique with the following variables used as instrumental variables: real wage (W/P), capital stock (K), the pre-tariff relative foreign price of imported inputs ($P^B*/P$), tariffs (TF), and a time trend. Equation (5.2) was not estimated because the actual data on gross output are not available and it would be inappropriate to use the estimated Q in a regression where Y and E, the elements in its estimate, are the only independent variables. The results of the estimated equations are reported in table 5.1. Unless otherwise stated, the numbers in parentheses below each coefficient are the t statistics. This convention will apply throughout this book.

In table 5.1, column 1.1 represents the Cobb-Douglas production function for value added, and columns 1.2 and 1.3 represent the demand functions for labour and imported inputs. A modified production function was also tried where domestic value added is expressed as a function of capital, labour and imported inputs. The specification was assumed to be Cobb-Douglas and was estimated in loglinear form. The estimated equation is reported in column 1.4.

## Table 5.1

### Estimates of production and input demand functions

| Column<br>Variable | 1.1<br>Y | 1.2<br>N | 1.3<br>E | 1.4<br>Y(Mod.) |
|---|---|---|---|---|
| Constant | -0.58<br>(-1.85) | 3.54<br>(3.88) | -2.29<br>(-1.77) | -0.82<br>(-2.24) |
| K | 0.30<br>(3.72) | 0.32<br>(0.06) | | 0.26<br>(3.14) |
| N | 0.82<br>(6.36) | | | 0.82<br>(6.21) |
| Q | | 0.89<br>(5.88) | 1.13<br>(6.73) | |
| E | | | | 0.08<br>(1.37) |
| W/P | | -0.55<br>(-3.36) | | |
| $P^E/P$ | | | -0.38<br>(-2.68) | |
| TF | | | -3.10<br>(-2.90) | |
| DW | 1.00 | 1.25 | 2.22 | 1.25 |
| Adj. $R^2$ | 0.99 | 0.97 | 0.81 | 0.99 |
| JB | 0.48 | 1.30 | 0.07 | 0.80 |
| ARCH | 1.01 | 0.70 | 4.72 | 0.97 |

Notes: DW, LM and JB are respectively the Durbin-Watson, Lagrange Multiplier and Jarque-Berra statistics. The critical values for the JB, LM, and the ARCH statistics are: 5.99, 3.84, and 5.99 respectively. The LM statistic was negative for all the equations implying the absence of autocorrelation. The numbers in the parentheses are t statistics.

The estimated parameters in table 5.1 support the production structure assumed. The overall fit of the regressions is very high as shown by the adjusted coefficients of determination ($R^{*2}$). The implied elasticities of output with respect to capital and labour (column 1.1) are 0.30 and 0.82 respectively and are statistically significant at the 5% level. Their sum is not significantly different from 1 as indicated by a calculated F statistic of 3.69, which is less than the critical value at the 1% level of significance. Therefore, the results support the assumption of constant returns to scale in the Cobb-Douglas production structure.

The parameter estimates of the factor demand functions turn out as expected. The coefficient of the real wage in the demand for labour function is fairly high at 0.55 and statistically significant at the 5% level. This is consistent with other studies of the Kenyan labour market which show that firms respond to labour market conditions (Killick 1981). The coefficient of capital also suggests that capital and labour are complementary but it is not statistically significant at the 5% level. The coefficient of gross output has the correct sign and is also statistically significant at the 5% level.

The coefficients of the imported input demand function are all statistically significant except for the constant term and have the expected signs. The coefficient of the tariff variable (TF) is -3.10 and is greater than the coefficient of the pre-tariff relative price of imported inputs (-0.38). This result supports Krueger's hypothesis regarding the importance of non-tariff barriers in the economy. She argued that if non-tariff barriers to imports were strengthened and weakened concurrently with changes in tariff barriers, the tariff variable should have a larger coefficient than the pre-tariff price of imported inputs (Krueger 1974).

Further, the coefficient of the imported input price is -0.38 and is statistically significant at the 5% level. From equation (5.4) above, this coefficient measures the elasticity of substitution between value added and imported inputs. We tested the hypothesis that this coefficient is not statistically different from 0.41, which was the direct estimate from equation (5.3) above. The computed F statistic is 0.04 and is less than the critical value at the 5% level of significance. As indicted earlier, this supports the structural features of the economy hypothesized in chapter 4.

The parameter estimates of the modified production function were not significantly different from the estimates in column 1.1. The respective coefficients for capital and labour are 0.26 and 0.82 and are statistically significant at the 5% level. But the coefficient of imported inputs is not significantly different from zero. The modified structure is not supported by Kenyan data.

The diagnostic tests do not suggest any serious econometric problem. The Jarque-Berra statistic is less than the critical value for all the equations, implying that the errors are normally distributed. The Durbin-Watson statistics for equations represented by columns 1.1, 1.2 and 1.3 fall between the critical lower and upper values of 0.98 and 1.30 at the 2.5% level and do not provide conclusive evidence of first order serial correlation. This is supported by the LM test which is negative and far less than the critical value. The LM test should, however, be interpreted with caution because it is an asymptotic test. The DW reported in column 1.4 does not suggest the presence of autocorrelation.

The results in table 5.1 answer some of the questions raised at the beginning of the chapter. The relative price elasticity of demand for imported inputs is -0.38 and is statistically significant at the 5% level. This confirms that external shocks which increase the price of imported inputs have significant and contractionary effects on the economy. These include exchange rate changes and exogenous increases in the foreign price of imports. As shown in equation (5.3), the coefficient of the relative price of imported inputs also measures the elasticity of substitution between imported inputs and value added. Its value of 0.38 is not significantly different from the value of 0.41 estimated from equation (5.3). The low elasticity of substitution is consistent with the hypothesis that there is limited substitution between imported inputs and domestic value added. Private producers are responsive to government tariff policy as indicated by the coefficient of the tariff variable. Therefore, Krueger's hypothesis (that if non-tariff barriers were strengthened and weakened concurrently with tariff barriers, the tariff variable should have a larger coefficient than the coefficient of the pre-tariff price of imported inputs) is supported by Kenyan data.

## 5.4 Private consumption

Our theoretical specification in chapter 4 assumed two types of consumers: workers and capitalists. Using the assumption that workers consume all their income, total workers' real consumption is estimated as the nominal wage bill deflated by the consumer price index. Capitalist consumption ($C_t^c$) is estimated from an intertemporal framework in accordance with recent developments in the theoretical and empirical literature. As noted in chapter 4, current empirical work on consumption is based on the Rational Expectations Permanent Income Hypothesis (REPIH) developed by Hall (1978) and extended by Flavin (1981). Studies applying this approach in developing countries have been undertaken by Zuelhke and Payne (1989),

Haque and Montiel (1989), Raut and Virmani (1989), and Rossi (1988). The methodology followed here draws from these studies. We start with an intertemporal utility function assumed to be additively separable over time. As assumed in chapter 4, each subperiod utility function is assumed to be strictly monotonic and concave. The capitalist consumer maximizes the following expected utility function:

$$EU = E_t \{ \Sigma_{j=0}^{\infty} (1+\tau)^{-j} u[C^c_{t+j}] \} \tag{5.6}$$

where:

| | |
|---|---|
| EU | expected value of intertemporal utility |
| u(.) | period utility function |
| $\tau$ | rate of time preference |
| $E_t(x)$ | expectations operator on a variable x conditional on the information available in period t |
| $C^c_t$ | consumption in period t |
| $\omega_t$ | wealth (value of assets) in period t |
| i | domestic rate of interest |

The information available in period t includes knowledge of the current and past values of consumption, wealth and the domestic interest rate. The rate of interest is assumed to be given exogenously to the consumer. The consumer's wealth is assumed to evolve according to the following equation:

$$\omega_{t+j} = \omega_t + i\omega_t + Y_t - C^c_t \tag{5.7}$$

The dynamic optimization of equation (5.6) subject to the constraint represented by equation (5.7) leads to the following Euler equation which characterizes optimal consumer behaviour:

$$u'[C^c_t] = (1+\tau)^{-j} E_t \{ \Sigma_{j=0}^{\infty} (1+\tau)^j u'[C^c_{t+j}] \} \tag{5.8}$$

This first order condition says that the consumer will maximize his utility when the marginal utility of consumption in period t, i.e., $U'[C^c_t]$, is equal to the expected marginal utility of consumption in period t+j, $E_t \{u'[C^c_{t+j}]\}$, appropriately adjusted by the discount rate and the rate of time preference. In a stochastic context, equation (5.8) implies that:

$$u'[C^c_{t+j}] = \{(1+\tau)/(1+i)\} u'[C^c_t] + \eta_{t+j} \tag{5.9}$$

76

where $\eta$ is the random error term assumed to have a zero mean and a constant variance. (5.9) implies that the rate of growth of marginal utility is equal to $(1+t)/(1+i)$. If $r=i$, marginal utility - and therefore consumption - will be constant over time except for a random error term. Consumption would therefore be a martingale (i.e., a random walk with drift).

To determine the level of consumption, the usual procedure is to first determine the permanently sustainable level of consumption which is the definition of 'permanent income' (Friedman 1957). Permanent income can be estimated as the rate of return on total human and nonhuman wealth (Abel 1990). If the rate of return on wealth is constant, fluctuations in permanent income are largely explained by unexpected fluctuations in human wealth. Hence, fluctuations in permanent income are due to revisions in expectations about future income.

To derive the form of the consumption function to be estimated, a constant elasticity of substitution (CES) function is often assumed in the literature.[1] Using this assumption, and for $j = 1$, the following relationship can be derived from the Euler relationship represented by equation (5.8) above:

$$\ln C^c_{t+1} - \ln C^c_t = C_0 + \Phi^{-1} E_t \ln(1+i_t)$$

$$+ \ln C^c_{t+1} - E_t \ln C^c_{t+1} \qquad (5.10)$$

where $\Phi^{-1}$ is the elasticity of substitution parameter (which is also the coefficient of relative risk aversion). With the constant interest rate assumed in this study, the second term of equation (5.10) is relegated to the constant term and a random walk consumption function is obtained. That is:

$$\Delta C^c_t = \lambda_0 + \lambda_1 \eta_t \qquad (5.11)$$

Equation (5.11) follows from the conclusions of the Hall-Flavin result that under rational expectations, consumption follows a random walk with drift and that no other variable should Granger-cause changes in consumption. According to Hall (1978), when consumers' expectations are rational, revisions to permanent income at time t are orthogonal to the information available at time t. Also, since consumption is proportional to permanent income, revisions to consumption are also orthogonal to the same information set. Moreover, unexpected changes in current income may cause revisions in permanent income and thus revisions in consumption (Flavin 1981). Consequently, only past consumption and unexpected income should be useful in predicting future consumption.

In the empirical literature, estimation of the random walk consumption function uses an alternative specification which encompasses the random walk hypothesis. This alternative specification expresses changes in consumption as a function of lagged consumption, expected and unexpected (or surprise) income. The following equation is usually estimated:

$$\Delta C^c_t = \beta_0 + \beta_1 C^c_{t-1} + \beta_2 Y^e_t + \beta_3 (Y_t - Y^e_t) + \epsilon_t \tag{5.12}$$

where:

| | |
|---|---|
| $\Delta$ | difference operator |
| $Y^e_t$ | expected income |
| $(Y_t - Y^e_t)$ | unexpected income (surprise component of income) |

In equation (5.12), lagged consumption captures habit persistence and expected income represents excess sensitivity effects associated with liquidity constraints (Flavin 1981). Under the null, the random walk hypothesis will hold if $\beta_2$ is statistically significant and $\beta_3$ is not. Some studies include current consumption as a regressor instead of lagged consumption in equation (5.12) (see, for example, Raut and Virmani 1989).

The expected and the unexpected components of income are unobservable. The usual method used to estimate models with such unobserved variables involves a two stage procedure where an equation (or a set of equations) representing the expectations mechanism of the unobserved variables is first estimated and constitutes the first stage of the estimation procedure. At the second stage, the residuals and the fitted values from the first regression are used as regressors in the consumption function to represent the unexpected and expected components respectively.

Pagan and Wickens (1989), and Pagan (1984) have discussed the econometric issues that arise when using generated variables as regressors. The procedure is asymptotically efficient and the standard errors of the surprise component of income can be estimated by applying the ordinary least squares technique to equation (5.12) above. The standard errors of the expected component, however, have to be estimated by applying the two stage least squares procedure to the model.

Alternative techniques used in the literature to deal with unobservable variables in rational expectations models are: the Instrumental Variables method (IV), and the Substitution Method (SM). The IV method was developed by Wickens (1982). He shows that for a wide range of models involving the rational expectation of regressors, consistent estimates can be obtained by replacing expected variables by their realized values and using exogenous and predetermined variables as instruments. In the SM method, the rationally expected variables are replaced by the estimates based on a restricted reduced form. The advantages of the IV method over the SM method are discussed in Wickens (1982). This book uses both the IV and the vector autoregression technique to distinguish between the expected and unexpected components.

Another econometric issue with implications for our study is the stationarity of time series data. Most empirical studies on consumption behaviour have noted that income and consumption data tend to be nonstationary in level form (Zulhke and Payne 1989). Standard inference procedures in econometrics depend on the assumption that the variables are stationary. The violation of this assumption invalidates the regression results. Although this is a crucial assumption, many studies on developing countries do not address this issue, mainly because the existing procedures are based on large sample sizes for which data are not usually available. Recent developments in the literature allow the testing for stationarity for any sample size (Mackinon 1990). The results of our tests suggest that when the series are in log form, there is no evidence of unit root. These results are reported in Appendix II.

There is no a priori procedure in the literature for determining the income generating process. Most studies assume income to follow an AR1 process (Hayashi 1985; Deaton 1987; Raut and Virmani 1989). Some other studies use lagged income and consumption to forecast income (Zulhke and Payne 1989). To facilitate comparisons with other studies, we shall estimate two cases: one where income follows an AR1 process, and another where income is determined by the first two lags of income and consumption. Both are summarized in the following equation:

$$Y_t = \alpha_0 + \alpha_2 Y_{t-1} + \alpha_3 C^c_{t-1} + \alpha_4 C^c_{t-2} + \mu_t \qquad (5.13)[2]$$

Equation (5.13) reduces to an AR1 process if: $\alpha_2 = \alpha_3 = \alpha_4 = 0$. In both cases, actual income is decomposed into an expected component (predicted income) $Y^e$, and an unexpected component $(Y-Y^e)$, which are then used as regressors in the estimation of equation (5.12). There are also other techniques for decomposing actual variables into expected and unexpected components. In fact, most studies seem to prefer the vector autoregression (VAR) technique. This book uses the two stage procedure explained above, as well as the VAR technique.

Table 5.2 provides parameter estimates of the REPIH consumption

79

function using the two stage procedure specified in equations (5.12) and (5.13) above. The forecasting equations for income are reported in columns 2.1 and 2.2, and the corresponding estimates of the consumption function are reported in columns 2.3 and 2.4. The consumption functions are specified as in Raut and Virmani (1989) and in Zulhke and Payne (1989) respectively. Also, the single equation estimates of columns 2.1 and 2.4 are identical to the corresponding VAR estimates. Therefore, VAR estimates are not separately reported.

The forecasting equations have a very high explanatory power as indicated by the adjusted coefficient of determination ($R^{*2}$ for each of the respective equations is 0.99 and 0.99). Except for the coefficients of $C^c_{t-1}$ and $Y_{t-2}$, the rest of the coefficients are statistically significant at the 5% level. This does not pose a serious problem since the two equations are used for forecasting purposes only. For the same reason we do not report the diagnostic tests for the forecasting equations. From column 2.3 of table 5.2, the parameter estimates are 0.47, -0.42 and 0.29 for $C^c_t$, $Y^e_t$ and $(Y-Y^e)$ respectively. All are statistically significant at the 5% level except for the coefficient of $(Y_t-Y^e)$. The corresponding estimates in Raut and Virmani are very small at 0.03, -0.003, and 0.01 and show the same pattern of statistical significance. The respective coefficients of $C^c_{t-1}$ and $Y^e_t$ in column 2.4 are: -0.40 and 0.43 and are statistically significant at the 10% level. The coefficient of $(Y_t-Y^e)$ is large (with a value of 1.80) and is statistically insignificant at the 10% level. In terms of magnitude and statistical significance of the coefficients, the results of column 2.4 differ from the work of Zulhke and Payne (1989).

The diagnostic statistics suggest the absence of serial correlation in both equations shown in columns 2.3 and 2.4. The respective DW, LM, and the ARCH statistics for the equations of columns 2.3 and 2.4 are: 1.92, 0.00, 0.90, and 1.84, 0.41, and 0.43. The estimated LM and ARCH values are below the critical values and thus reject the hypothesis of serial correlation. The DW statistics are very close to 2.00 indicating no first order autocorrelation and heteroscedasticity. Also the JB statistic for both equations is respectively 1.07 and 2.19, which are less than their critical values. This supports the assumption of normality in the error terms.

## Table 5.2

## Parameter estimates of the REPIH consumption function
### (equations 5.12 and 5.13)

| Column<br>Variable | 2.1<br>$Y_t$ | 2.2<br>$Y_t$ | 2.3<br>$\Delta C_t^c$ | 2.4<br>$\Delta C_t^c$ |
|---|---|---|---|---|
| Constant | 0.20<br>(1.56) | 0.38<br>(3.68) | 0.09<br>(0.20) | -0.53<br>(-0.97) |
| $Y_{t-1}$ | 0.98<br>(55.42) | 0.66<br>(4.18) | | |
| $Y_{t-2}$ | | 0.22<br>(1.42) | | |
| $C_t^c$ | | | 0.47<br>(2.67) | |
| $C_{t-1}^c$ | | -0.02<br>(-0.53) | | -0.40<br>(-1.96) |
| $C_{t-2}^c$ | | 0.11<br>(2.22) | | |
| $Y_t^e$ | | | -0.42<br>(-2.25) | 0.43<br>(2.00) |
| $Y_t - Y_t^e$ | | | 0.29<br>(0.40) | 1.80<br>(1.53) |
| Adj. $R^2$ | 0.99 | 0.99 | 0.19 | 0.13 |
| SER | 0.03 | 0.02 | 0.10 | 0.10 |
| DW | | | 1.92 | 1.84 |
| LM | | | 0.00 | 0.41 |
| ARCH | | | 0.90 | 0.43 |
| JB | | | 1.07 | 2.19 |

Notes: Diagnostic tests are not provided for the forecasting equations in columns 2.1 and 2.2. SER is the standard error of the regression; other abbreviations and critical values are as in table 5.1.

However, the overall F statistics for both equations of columns 2.3 and 2.4 are less than their critical values. The estimated values are 2.83 and 2.12 which are less than the critical value of 3.10. This suggests that the specification of consumption in equations (5.12) and (5.13) is inadequate for Kenya. This is very different from the studies by Raut and Virmani (1989), and Zulhke and Payne (1989) which reject the REPIH but not the specification of the estimating equation.

The low levels of significance of the regressions in table 5.2, together with the low coefficients of determination, for the consumption equations suggest that some variables which influence consumption behaviour in Kenya were omitted from the specification. As a result, we attempted an alternative and more general model. Following Blinder and Deaton (1985), the following equation was specified:

$$C^c_t = \gamma_0 + \gamma_1 C^c_{t-1} + \gamma_2 Y_t + \gamma_3 Y_{t-1} + \gamma_j Z_t + \nu_t \qquad (5.14)$$

where $Z_t$ includes other current and lagged variables that are expected to influence consumption behaviour. In our case the variables included under $Z_t$ are: government expenditure $(G_t)$, the real exchange rate $(R_t)$, and the capacity to import $(IM_t)$. The subscript j represents the coefficients of the variables included in $Z_t$. In equation (5.14), current income captures the effect of liquidity constraints. The rationale for including government expenditure is based on the argument that government expenditures may substitute for or complement private consumption. Government expenditures were found to be important in determining consumer behaviour by Rossi (1988). The real exchange rate was shown to have an effect on consumption in chapter 4. The capacity to import is used as a proxy for the effect of external economic factors (shocks). This is a major determinant of private expenditures in many small open economies whose GDP is strongly influenced by international market conditions.

As in our earlier equations, the contemporaneously dated variables are decomposed into expected and unexpected components. The null hypothesis is still the same; only unexpected components should be statistically significant if agents have rational expectations. The contemporaneously dated variables are considered endogenous and have to be predicted using all the information available at time t. Blinder and Deaton (1985) have shown that a model that includes both expected and unexpected components is observationally equivalent to one where the equation similar to equation (5.12) above is estimated using the two stage least squares method. One can therefore choose between the two approaches. In line with recent studies, we use the approach which distinguishes between the predicted and the unpredicted (surprise) variables.

To decompose the variables into predicted and unpredicted components, we use a VAR technique where all the endogenous variables are expressed as functions of the lagged endogenous variables and the exogenous variables of the system. The estimates from the VAR system are then used to decompose the variables into predicted and unpredicted variables. The following specification is adopted:

$$
\begin{bmatrix} Y_t \\ C^c_t \\ Z_t \end{bmatrix} = \begin{bmatrix} AA(L) & AB(L) & AC(L) \\ BA(L) & BB(L) & BC(L) \\ CA(L) & CB(L) & CC(L) \end{bmatrix} \begin{bmatrix} Y_t \\ C^c_t \\ Z_t \end{bmatrix} = \begin{bmatrix} v_{1t} \\ v_{2t} \\ v_{3t} \end{bmatrix} \qquad (5.15)
$$

where AA(L), AB(L), AC(L), BA(L), BB(L), BC(L), CA(L), CB(L) and CC(L) are polynomials in the lag operator L [ e.g. $AA(L) = a_1 L + a_2 L^2 + \ldots + a_n L^n$]; $Y_t$ and $C^c_t$ are as defined before; $Z_t$ includes all the other variables that may have an influence on consumption. $v_{1t}$, $v_{2t}$ and $v_{3t}$ are random errors assumed to be independently distributed across time but may be contemporaneously correlated.

The VAR estimates for $Y_t$, $G_t$, $R_t$, and $IM_t$ are reported in table 5.3. These estimates are used to construct the predicted and unpredicted variables which are then used to estimate the consumption function of equation (5.14). This two stage procedure where the estimated VARS are used to construct the predicted and unpredicted variables is favoured over other system methods which estimate equations (5.14) and (5.15) simultaneously (Blinder and Deaton 1985, p.476). However, the estimated standard errors are imprecise because the technique treats both predicted and the unpredicted series as known data.

Pagan (1984) and Wickens (1982) have recommended that the standard errors of the coefficients should be estimated in a two stage least squares procedure where the unpredicted variables are omitted and equation (5.14) is estimated using a VAR method at the first stage. The parameter estimates of the consumption function specified in equation (5.14) are reported in table 5.4.

Column 4.1 of table 5.4 reports the parameter estimates of the general specification of private consumption for Kenya. Lagged consumption $C^c_{t-1}$ has a large and statistically significant effect on private consumption as indicated by the elasticity of 1.41. This result supports the idea that consumers tend to smoothen consumption over time by adjusting current consumption in relation to past consumption. The coefficient of lagged income is also large but is statistically insignificant. The coefficients of the expected components of income ($Y^e_t$), expected government expenditure ($G^e_t$), and the expected real exchange rate ($R^e_t$); are also statistically significant at the 5% level. The capacity to import coefficient is significant at the 10% level.

Expected income has a positive effect on consumption of 6.10. The sign is as expected but contrary to the rational expectations assumption, the coefficient is statistically different from 0. A 1% increase in expected government expenditures ($G^e_t$) and expected real exchange rate ($R^e_t$) reduces private consumption by 2.33 and 9.39 respectively. The effect of exogenous shocks on consumption is large as indicated by the magnitude of the coefficient but its low statistical significance suggests that these external effects are not dominant.

These results suggest that government expenditure substitutes for private consumption. This is not unusual for an economy like Kenya where the government has subsidized private spending for a long time. The theoretical analysis in chapter 4 showed that the effect of real exchange rate appreciation on consumption is indeterminate. The empirical results show that the negative effect dominates.

The coefficients of the surprise components of the explanatory variables are smaller than their corresponding expected components. For the four variables, they are smaller than their corresponding expected components by more than 50%. The respective magnitudes of the coefficients are: -2.81, 0.62, -1.13, and -0.37 for ($Y_t$-$Y^e_t$), ($G_t$-$G^e_t$), ($R_t$-$R^e_t$) and ($IM_t$-$IM^e_t$). Except for the surprise component of the real exchange rate with a strong statistical significance at 5%, the other coefficients of the surprise variables are only significant at the 10% level.

The overall significance of the regression is very high with an F value of 6.13 compared to a critical value of 4.84 with 12 degrees of freedom. The adjusted coefficient of determination is relatively high at 0.70. There is no evidence of autocorrelation as indicated by the DW statistic of 1.92. Also, the ARCH test suggests that there is no evidence of heteroscedasticity. The JB statistic for testing normality has a value of 1.89 which is less than the critical value of 5.99. The inferences drawn from table 5.4 are therefore supported by the diagnostic tests.

## Table 5.3

### Decomposition of explanatory variables into expected and unexpected components (using VAR Techniques)

| Column | 3.1 | 3.2 | 3.3 | 3.4 |
|---|---|---|---|---|
| Variable | $Y_t$ | $G_t$ | $R_t$ | $IM_t$ |
| Constant | 0.13 | -3.52 | 3.22 | 0.03 |
| | (0.25) | (-1.58) | (1.70) | (0.01) |
| $C^e_{t-1}$ | -0.15 | -0.18 | 0.29 | -0.45 |
| | (-2.32) | (-0.63) | (1.24) | (-1.15) |
| $C^e_{t-2}$ | 0.12 | -0.02 | 0.01 | 0.61 |
| | (2.55) | (-0.08) | (0.05) | (2.14) |
| $Y_{t-1}$ | 0.61 | 0.57 | -0.50 | 0.01 |
| | (3.57) | (0.73) | (-0.79) | (0.01) |
| $Y_{t-2}$ | 0.52 | 0.28 | -0.11 | -0.19 |
| | (2.75) | (0.33) | (-0.16) | (-0.16) |
| $G_{t-1}$ | 0.04 | 0.30 | -0.22 | 0.26 |
| | (0.57) | (0.93) | (-0.83) | (0.60) |
| $G_{t-2}$ | -0.14 | 0.10 | 0.43 | -0.33 |
| | (-1.79) | (0.24) | (1.48) | (-0.69) |
| $R_{t-1}$ | -0.19 | -0.08 | 0.61 | 0.52 |
| | (-2.28) | (-0.22) | (2.02) | (1.05) |
| $R_{t-2}$ | 0.12 | -0.00 | -0.10 | 0.30 |
| | (1.28) | (-0.01) | (-0.28) | (0.52) |
| $IM_{t-1}$ | 0.01 | 0.19 | -0.04 | 0.39 |
| | (0.17) | (0.80) | (-0.23) | (1.24) |
| $IM_{t-2}$ | 0.21 | 0.18 | -0.11 | 0.43 |
| | (0.02) | (0.84) | (-0.65) | (1.52) |
| Adj. $R^2$ | 0.99 | 0.95 | 0.67 | 0.67 |

Note: Diagnostic tests are not provided in this table since these equations are used for forecasting purposes only.

Table 5.4

**Parameter estimates of private consumption using VAR techniques to decompose explanatory variables into expected and unexpected components**

| Column<br>Variable: | 4.1<br>$\Delta C^c_t$ | 4.2<br>$\Delta C^c_t$ |
|---|---|---|
| Constant | -3.78<br>(-0.36) | -5.35<br>(-0.52) |
| $C^e_{t-1}$ | -1.41<br>(-7.09) | -1.37<br>(-7.05) |
| $Y_{t-1}$ | -1.50<br>(-0.98) | |
| $Y^e_t$ | 6.10<br>(4.66) | 5.05<br>(6.71) |
| $(Y_t-Y^e_t)$ | -2.81<br>(-1.84) | -3.36<br>(-2.37) |
| $G^e_t$ | -2.33<br>(-5.17) | 2.44<br>(-5.60) |
| $(G_t-G^e_t)$ | 0.62<br>(1.88) | 0.55<br>(1.70) |
| $IM_t$ | 1.53<br>(1.86) | 1.51<br>(1.84) |
| $(IM_t-IM^e_t)$ | -0.37<br>(-1.62) | -0.19<br>(-1.37) |
| $R^e_t$ | -9.39<br>(-2.95) | -8.37<br>(-2.76) |
| $(R_t-R^e_t)$ | -1.13<br>(-3.15) | -0.99<br>(-3.01) |
| | | |
| Adj. $R^2$ | 0.70 | 0.70 |
| SER | 0.06 | 0.06 |
| DW | 1.92 | 1.94 |
| LM | 6.72 | 4.71 |
| ARCH | 2.63 | 0.85 |
| JB | 1.89 | 1.30 |

Notes: Column 4.2 omits $Y_{t-1}$ since its t statistic was statistically insignificant at the 5% level.

The strong statistical significance of the expected components of $Y_t$, $G_t$, $R_t$ and $IM_t$ lead to the rejection of the rational expectations hypothesis that only unexpected components are statistically significant in explaining consumption. This result is reinforced by the relatively weak statistical significance of the unexpected components. We tested for the hypothesis that only the unexpected components are statistically different from 0. The computed F statistic with 12 degrees of freedom was 4.06 which is larger than the critical value of 3.36, rejecting the hypothesis at the 5% level of significance. We therefore concluded that both expected and unexpected components are important in explaining consumption behaviour in Kenya.

Also, we tested for the hypothesis that the coefficient of $Y_{t-1}$ is not statistically different from 0. The calculated F statistic was 0.97 compared to the critical value of 4.84 with 12 degrees of freedom. The null hypothesis could not be rejected at the 5% level and lagged income was dropped from the regression. The estimated regression excluding lagged income is reported in column 4.2 of table 5.4. The estimated parameters show no significant change from those of the previous equation which includes lagged income.

Hence, the Kenyan data support the specification reported in column 4.2 of table 5.4. The empirical and theoretical literature has several explanations for the rejection of the rational expectations hypothesis that only unexpected components should be significant in explaining consumption behaviour. The strong significance of current income for current consumption is known as the 'excess-sensitivity' of consumption (Flavin 1981). This excess sensitivity can be due to the liquidity constraints associated with imperfect capital markets, which can be explained in terms of the moral hazard problems associated with lending. We have already noted in chapter 4 that such liquidity constraints are part of the institutional features of the Kenyan economy. Further, the response to the uncertainty of incomes, consumption needs and the date of death, may not be properly captured in the expected utility hypothesis. If it is not, then the rational expectations expected utility hypothesis of consumption would not perform well for Kenya, where the uncertainty of farm and other incomes is pervasive.

## 5.5 Private investment

The theoretical foundations of our investment model are based on the neoclassical framework of the intertemporal dynamic optimization of the present discounted value of expected profits, subject to the underlying technology. The following formulation is usually adopted:

$$\text{Max.: } \int_0^\infty e^{-it} [P.Y - W.N - P_I.I] \, \Delta t \qquad (5.16)$$

$$\text{subject to: } \quad Y = F(K,N)$$

where $P^I$ is the price of investment goods and all the other variables are as defined before. Using the concept of the user cost of capital and in the absence of adjustment costs, Jorgenson (1963) has shown that the optimization of equation (5.16) can be reduced to the static case. However, in the presence of adjustment costs, the user cost of capital has to be redefined.

Zagame (1977) has shown that even in the presence of adjustment costs, the demand for the capital stock derived from equation (5.16) is identical to the one obtained from a static framework but with the user cost of capital redefined to take into account the adjustment costs. Muet (1990) used this framework to analyze investment demand using annual data for France. He showed that a general specification can be derived which encompasses three main theories of investment. These are: the notional (or pure) neoclassical model, the effective demand constraint model, and the financial constraints model. The main distinction is in the constraints that firms face and therefore the explanatory variables that enter into the determination of investment. Muet argued that in a macroeconomic context, it is possible for all the constraints to be observed jointly. He concluded that the macroeconomic investment function should depend simultaneously on all the explanatory variables (p. 51).

We shall draw on Muet's general specification to analyze investment behaviour in Kenya. We assume an additive log-linear relationship of the following form:

$$(I/K)_t = a_0 + a_1 Y^e_t + a_2 (P^K/W)^e_t + a_3 I^g_t$$

$$+ a_4 R^e_t + a_5 IM_t + \varsigma_t \qquad (5.17)$$

where:

| | |
|---|---|
| $Y^e$ | expected sales |
| $(P^K/W)^e$ | expected relative factor prices |
| $I^g$ | government investment |
| $R^e$ | expected real exchange rate |
| $\varsigma$ | white noise |

According to the pure neoclassical model, only relative factor prices would be statistically significant in equation (5.17). Expected sales take into account the fact that firms may be demand constrained. Demand constraints were found to be a major factor determining investment decisions in Kenya by Coughlin and Ikiara (1988). The real exchange rate was shown to be one of the variables affecting investment in chapter 4.

IM represents the capacity of the economy to import and is defined as the total value of export earnings deflated by the import price index. This variable is used as a proxy for variables like foreign exchange constraints, the availability of credit and profitability. The justification for this is that in a developing country with severe foreign exchange constraints like Kenya, the capacity to import determines the extent to which foreign exchange controls and the credit squeeze to the private sector are relaxed. The capacity to import is therefore expected to be positively correlated with the easing of credit and foreign exchange controls. This means that an improvement in the capacity to import would increase private investment.

Government investment was included in equation (5.17) as an explanatory variable to test the crowding out hypothesis. The effect of government investment is *a priori* ambiguous and can only be determined empirically. The theoretical argument is that certain types of public investment crowd out private investment, especially if they compete for scarce capital resources or if their output competes with private sector output. Other types of public investment such as infrastructure stimulate private investment (Blejer and Khan 1984).

As for the consumption function, rational expectations is the maintained hypothesis. Equation (5.16) involves unobserved variables and is estimated using both the instrumental variables technique and the two stage method which distinguishes between expected and unexpected components. As noted in section 5.3, models involving the rational expectation of variables can be estimated using the instrumental variables technique where the rationally expected variables are replaced with their actual values and the equation is estimated using instrumental variables. The results of the two stage model with both expected and unexpected components of variables used as regressors turned out to be very poor and unstable. Except for the coefficient on expected income, all the other coefficients were statistically insignificant. The results for this model using the instrumental variable technique are not reported here.

The estimated parameters of equation (5.16) using the Two Stage Least Squares (TSLS) are reported in table 5.5. It was assumed that government expenditure and the real exchange rate are predetermined. This is in line with our hypothesis that the government and private agents play a Stackleberg game with the government acting as the leader. This hypothesis is tested in section

5.6 below. The following variables were used in table 5.5 as instrumental variables: $I^g_t$, $I^g_{t-1}$, $Y_{t-1}$, $R_t$, $R_{t-1}$, $IM_t$, $(P^K/W)_t$, $FP^E_t$ and $FP^E_{t-1}$. $FP^E_t$ is the foreign price of imported inputs.

From table 5.5, the investment equation fits the data well and has a high explanatory power in terms of the adjusted coefficient of determination ($R^{*2} = 0.85$). The coefficient of expected sales is very strong at 2.83 and is statistically significant at the 5% level. The capacity to import, which represents external shocks to the economy, has a positive and statistically significant coefficient of 0.64. This reflects the crucial importance of exogenous effects such as foreign exchange shortages and increases in the price of imports in determining investment in Kenya. Our results are consistent with the findings of the Industrial Research Project of the University of Nairobi (Coughlin and Ikiara 1988). Their findings showed that the two main constraints on investors' decision to invest were foreign exchange availability and expected sales.

The theoretical model of chapter 4 showed that the real exchange rate has a negative effect on private investment. The coefficient of this variable is 0.73 but it is only significant at the 10% level. The relatively weak effect of the real exchange rate is not surprising, given that the government did not pursue an active exchange rate policy for most of the period under study (Gulhati *et al* 1984).

The effect of government investment on private investment is negative. Based on our results, a 1% increase in government expenditure reduces private investment by 0.86%. This suggests that in the case of Kenya, government investment crowds out private investment. The Ndegwa Commission on the consequences of high government deficits suggested that they had a negative effect on private sector investment (Ndegwa 1982). The investment equation estimated here is consistent with the Commission's conclusions.

The diagnostic tests performed on the estimated equation in table 5.5 do not suggest any serious econometric problem. This supports the inferences drawn from the estimated parameters. The DW statistic of 1.86 suggests the absence of serial correlation. This is consistent with the Lagrange Multiplier test which, with an estimated coefficient of 0.14, is less than the critical value of 3.84. Similarly, the ARCH statistic and the Jarque-Berra test have estimates that are less than their critical values.

## Table 5.5

### Parameter estimates of private investment
### (using Two Stage Least Squares)

| Column | 5.1 |
| --- | --- |
| Constant | -25.71 |
| | (-2.63) |
| $Y_t$ | 2.83 |
| | (2.07) |
| $I^g_t$ | -1.04 |
| | (-2.40) |
| $(P^K/W)_t$ | -0.87 |
| | (-2.59) |
| $R_t$ | -0.73 |
| | (-1.74) |
| $IM_t$ | 0.64 |
| | (2.02) |
| Adj. $R^2$ | 0.85 |
| SER | 0.13 |
| DW | 1.86 |
| LM | 0.14 |
| ARCH | 0.73 |
| JB | 2.80 |

## 5.6 Government behaviour

Chapter 4 noted that the government's social welfare function depends on the private sector behaviour, government policy, and the exogenous variables of the system. Using a similar specification as in Conway (1987), this can be represented by the following reduced form:

$$\underline{G}_t = \underline{G}_t,\ \underline{Y}^g_t,\ \underline{X}^g_t,\ \underline{K}^g_t,\ \underline{\zeta}_t) \tag{5.18}$$

where:

| | |
|---|---|
| $\underline{G}$ | vector of governmental policy variables |
| $\underline{Y}^g$ | vector of private sector choices |
| $\underline{X}^g$ | vector of all exogenous variables |
| $\underline{K}^g$ | vector of predetermined state variables |
| $\underline{\zeta}$ | vector of white noise terms |

The policy choices considered in this book as being available to the government are: government consumption, government investment, exchange rate policy, tariff policy and monetary policy. Private sector behaviour is represented by output supply, private consumption, and private investment. The following variables are considered to be exogenous to government behaviour: foreign prices of imported inputs and exports, changes in the demand for exports, and changes in the foreign cost of borrowing. All these exogenous shocks had significant effects on government policies in the developing countries in the 1970s and 1980s (Balassa 1982).

In its analysis of government behaviour, this book is concerned with two main issues: whether the government's policy responses to exogenous shocks were as predicted by our theory; and the nature of the interaction between the government and the private sector. The former is considered below in this section and the latter is analyzed in the next section.

The model of chapter 4 predicted that given the social welfare function, the government would respond to exogenous shocks by undertaking policy measures to counteract the negative effects of the shock. For instance, following an increase in the foreign currency price of imported inputs, the government would appreciate the real exchange rate. Appreciating the exchange rate minimizes the negative impact of the shock on private production and employment. It should be noted that the appreciation of the exchange rate could arise from the government's fiscal and monetary policies. Increasing government spending with deficit financing can cause inflation if the deficit is money financed. This would then lead to an appreciation of the exchange rate. If the government responds to an external shock by financing its spending this way, the real exchange rate would appreciate. In fact, in Kenya, deficit financing through borrowing from the Central Bank of Kenya has been one of the main causes of inflation (Killick 1984).

As argued in Conway (1987, p.124), if government policy responds to the external shock, then the surprise (or unexpected) component of the shock should have a statistically significant effect on unexpected changes in government policy. Given the small country assumption, causation runs from exogenous shock surprises to government policy surprises. Conway tested for this hypothesis by regressing government policy surprises on the unexpected component of the shock. His specification however considered the effect of only one exogenous shock, i.e., an increase in the price of imported inputs. This ignores the possibility of a simultaneous occurrence of shocks and a simultaneous policy response to more than one shock which is more in line with reality. This book takes these into account by regressing each policy surprise on all the exogenous shock surprises.

The exogenous shocks considered here are: an increase in the foreign currency price of imported inputs, an increase in the foreign interest rate, a change in the foreign demand for exports, and changes in the foreign currency price of exports. All the variables are denominated in foreign currency to reflect the fact that it is the foreign components that are exogenous. The government is taken to be able to change domestic prices through its policies.

In the empirical literature on the developed economies, the surprise components are generated by computing deviations from the steady state or long run, optimal, shock free solution of the model. In the case of developing countries, this long run steady state solution of the model is not a reasonable representation of reality. Instead, we follow what other studies in developing countries have done by generating a time path of the economy under favourable assumptions regarding economic developments.[3] Specifically, the time path of external shocks and government policy variables are generated under the assumption that these continue to grow at the same trend as in the pre-shock period.[4] The surprise components are computed by subtracting the actual values of the variables from the pre-shock trend values.

In Kenya, the first serious external shock since independence occurred in 1973 when oil prices almost doubled (Killick 1984). The period between 1964 and 1972 is, therefore, used to estimate the trend parameters of the following equation:

$$\psi_t = a \, \psi_{t-1}^\delta \tag{5.19}$$

where $\psi$ represents the exogenous and government policy variables in the analysis. The parameters a and $\delta$ are estimated using ordinary least squares regression. The estimated coefficients are then used to generate the trend values of the exogenous shocks and government policy variables. The results of the regressions of government policy surprises on exogenous shock surprises are reported in table 5.6.

The results reported in table 5.6 show that the government was responsive to external shocks. Imported input price surprises have statistically significant effects on the surprise components of government consumption, tariff policy and monetary policy, with coefficients of 0.33, -0.32, and 0.11 respectively. The effect on exchange rate policy surprise of -0.10 is statistically significant at the 10% level. Foreign export demand surprises have statistically significant coefficients of 0.48, 1.54, -0.66 and 0.75 on government consumption, investment, exchange rate and monetary policy surprises respectively. These results suggest that the government was very concerned with changes in the foreign price of imported inputs and changes in the value of exports. The signs of the coefficients are as predicted in chapter 4.

Foreign interest rate surprises have significant effects on investment and tariff policy surprises only. Foreign export price surprises do not appear to have significant effects on the government's policy choices. The reason for this could be that their effects are captured in the variable representing the value of exports.

There is no evidence of serial correlation as shown by the DW and LM statistics except for column 6.5 in table 5.6. Similarly, the ARCH test suggests no heteroscedasticity. The JB test for normality supports the assumption of normally distributed error terms. Valid inferences can therefore be made from the estimated parameters.

## 5.7 The interaction between the government and the private sector

The interaction between the government and the private sector depends on the structure of the game as noted in chapter 4. We assumed a non-cooperative game structure with two possible timing structures: a concurrent timing structure and a Stackleberg timing structure where the government is the leader. Using the same reasoning as in section 5.6 above, the concurrent timing structure implies that only private sector surprises are statistically significant in an equation explaining government policy. Also, if the government was a Stackleberg leader, the same result would follow because it does not know the private sector choices before formulating policy. We test the hypothesis that the interaction between the two is characterized by a concurrent structure against the alternative that it is not.

To derive the surprise components of private sector choices, we follow the same procedure as in section 5.6 above. Base values are generated assuming that the trend growth of the variables continued at the pre-shock trend growth rates. The year 1973 was chosen to mark the onset of the first major external shock to the economy. The estimated results are presented in table 5.7. The following government policies are considered: government consumption, government investment, tariff policy, exchange rate policy, and monetary policy. These policy variables are regressed on the following explanatory variables and private sector surprises: the foreign prices of imported inputs and capital; private investment and gross output supply surprises.

From the available evidence, government investment, exchange rate and monetary policies suggest a Stackleberg leader hypothesis. The response of the three policies to private sector investment surprises are statistically significant and have the expected signs. The respective coefficients are: 0.55, -0.47 and 0.40. Therefore, in the case of private investment surprises, we cannot reject the null hypothesis that the government was Stackleberg leader. These results are consistent with the finding in section 5.4 that current government investment has a significant effect on private investment. This would be the case if the private sector was a follower and the government was the leader.

The gross output supply surprises are statistically significant in explaining all the government policies considered. This suggests a concurrent timing structure or a Stackleberg leader game structure where the private sector is the leader. The overall results are mixed, suggesting that in this case the interaction between the government and the private sector can be either of the two structures assumed, depending on the objectives of the government and the type of policy used.[5]

## Table 5.6

### The effects of exogenous shock surprises on governmental policy surprises

| Column<br>Variable | 6.1<br>SGC | 6.2<br>SGI | 6.3<br>SREX | 6.4<br>STRF | 6.5<br>SRMP |
|---|---|---|---|---|---|
| Const. | -0.12<br>(-1.52) | 0.06<br>(0.39) | 0.12<br>(1.38) | 0.14<br>(0.63) | 0.02<br>(0.21) |
| SPE | 0.33<br>(6.63) | -0.01<br>(-0.16) | -0.10<br>(-1.75) | -0.32<br>(-2.31) | 0.11<br>(2.26) |
| SUSX | 0.48<br>(2.20) | 1.54<br>(3.93) | -0.66<br>(-2.73) | 0.39<br>(0.64) | 0.75<br>(3.66) |
| SUSI | -0.09<br>(-0.69) | 0.45<br>(2.03) | 0.03<br>(0.19) | 0.70<br>(2.01) | -0.19<br>(-1.64) |
| SUSPX | 0 07<br>(0.83) | 0.15<br>(1.00) | -0.23<br>(-2.54) | o 05<br>(0.22) | 0.07<br>(0.97) |
| Adj. $R^2$ | 0.86 | 0.52 | 0.53 | 0.38 | 0.81 |
| DW | 1.79 | 1.77 | 1.66 | 2.22 | 2.59 |
| JB | 1.79 | 1.15 | 0.55 | 0.97 | 0.65 |
| LM | 0.08 | 1.12 | 0.47 | 0.80 | 1.59 |
| ARCH | 0.29 | 3.45 | 4.65 | 2.20 | 2.51 |

Notes: SGC, SGI, SREX, SREX, SRTF, and SRMP represent the surprise components of government consumption, government investment, real exchange rate, tariff policy, and monetary policy respectivelly. SPE, SUSX, SUSI and SUSPX are the respective surprise components of the price of imported inputs, foreign demand for exports, foreign interest rates, and the foreign price of exports.

## Table 5.7

### Governmental policy responses to private sector responses

| column var. | 7.1 $C^g$ | 7.2 $I^g$ | 7.3 TR | 7.4 R | 7.5 $M^s$ |
|---|---|---|---|---|---|
| Cons. | 6.20 (83.00) | 5.39 (32.78) | -1.64 (-7.24) | 1.83 (24.54) | 7.00 (100.97) |
| $P*^E/P$ | 0.26 (2.62) | 0.32 (1.52) | -0.17 (-0.60) | -0.26 (-2.65) | -0.22 (-2-45) |
| $P*^K/P$ | 0.28 (11.51) | 0.11 (2.15) | 0.15 (2.06) | -0.04 (1.69) | -0.28 (-12.29) |
| PISUP | 0.21 (1-72) | 0.55 (2-01) | -0.14 (-0.37) | -0.47 (-3.79) | 0.40 (3.50) |
| QSUP | 0.22 (0.60) | 0.83 (1.00) | -1.29 (-1.13) | -0.13 (0.33) | 0.19 (0.56) |
| Adj. $R^2$ | 0.93 | 0.44 | 0.39 | 0.71 | 0.93 |
| D.W. | 1.93 | 2.14 | 1.89 | 2.74 | 2.97 |
| JB | 0.61 | 1.01 | 0.35 | 0.30 | 0.91 |
| LM | 0.00 | 0.35 | 0.01 | 2.93 | 6.31 |

Note: $P*^E/P$ and $P*^K/P$ are the relative foreign prices of imported inputs, and capital respectively.

## Conclusions

This chapter has provided empirical evidence for the theoretical model developed in chapter 4 and to provide answers to the questions raised in the introductory section of this chapter. Most of the findings support the predictions of our theoretical model. For example, we found that private producers responded to external shocks by reducing their demand for imported inputs to maximize profits. The effects of an increase in the price of imported inputs is therefore contractionary. Also, the elasticity of substitution between imported inputs and domestic value added is low but statistically different from zero. This result is consistent with the structural features of the Kenyan economy discussed in chapter 4.

These two findings reject the structuralist argument that private producers are not responsive to imported input price increases and that the elasticity of substitution between imported inputs and domestic value added is equal to zero. Therefore, the structuralist explanation for the persistence of current account deficits is not supported by the empirical evidence in Kenya.

The government responses to external shocks were found to be as predicted by theory. For instance, following an increase in the foreign currency price of imported inputs, the government would appreciate the real exchange rate or undertake policies - such as deficit financing through borrowing from the central bank - that would lead to an indirect appreciation of the real exchange rate. The main reason for this policy response was assumed to be the government's desire to counteract the negative effects of the external shocks. This, however, worsens the current account. Therefore, we conclude that the persistence of current account deficits is largely due to government policies (see Conway (1987) for a similar finding for Turkey).

Although the Rational Expectations Permanent Income Hypothesis was rejected for Kenya, this does not imply that private agents in Kenya do not form their expectations rationally. As explained in section 5.3, the failure of this hypothesis could be due to factors other than the rational formation of expectations. Further, the estimates of consumption which do not distinguish between the expected and unexpected components (as in the Instrumental Variables approach) appear to explain the data equally well. We cannot, therefore, determine the relative significance of either the Instrumental Variables approach or the two stage estimation procedure (which makes a distinction between the expected and unexpected components).

Based on the estimated parameters, the interaction between the government and the private sector can be modelled either as a non-cooperative Stackleberg game with the government as the leader or a non-cooperative

Nash structure depending on the type of policy. In the case of government investment spending, the Stackleberg hypothesis with the government as the leader cannot be rejected. However, with respect to government consumption, a concurrent timing structure or a Stackleberg structure with the private sector as the leader cannot be rejected.

In conclusion, we note that the interaction between the government and the private sector plays an important role in influencing the current account. Hence, it is necessary to distinguish the relative contribution of government policy in explaining the persistence of current account deficits. This is the objective of the next chapter.

## Appendix I

## Derivation of factor demand functions

Given:
$$Q = [dY^\rho + (1-d)E^\rho]^{1/\rho} \tag{1}$$

$$Y = K^\alpha N^{(1-\alpha)} \tag{2}$$

Substituting equation (2) into (1) yields:

$$Q^\rho = [d(K^\alpha N^{1-\alpha})^\rho + (1-d)E^\rho] \tag{3}$$

Taking total differentials:

$$\rho a Q^{\rho-1} \Delta Q = \rho \alpha a K^{(1-\alpha)} N^{\rho\alpha-1} \Delta N + \rho(1-a) E^{\rho-1} \Delta E \tag{4}$$

Equating the marginal products of labour and imported inputs with their respective marginal products, the respective factor demands can be derived as follows:

$$MPN = \alpha dK^{(1-\alpha)\rho} N^{\rho\alpha-1} Q^{1-\rho} = (W/P) \tag{5}$$

$$MPE = (1-d) E^{\rho-1} Q^{1-\rho} = (P^E /P) \tag{6}$$

where MPN and MPE are the marginal products of labour and capital respectively. Equation (6) can be rewritten as follows:

$$(1-d).(Q/E)^{(1-\rho)} = P^E/P \tag{7}$$

Taking logs of equation (7) and rearranging:

$$\ln(Q/E) = \ln(1-d) + 1/(1-\rho) \ln(P^E/P) \tag{8}$$

Differentiating equation (8) yields the elasticity of substitution as,

$$d\ln(Q/E)/d\ln(P^E/P) = 1/(1-\rho)$$

Equation (8) is similar to equation (3) and is used to estimate the elasticity of substitution between value added and imported inputs.

The demand functions derived from equations (5) and (6) are:

$$N = (W/P)^{\beta} K^{\beta'} Q^{\beta''} C \tag{9}$$

$$E = (P^E/P)^{1/(\sigma-1)} Q \tag{10}$$

where:

$$\beta = [\sigma/(\sigma-(\sigma-1)\alpha]$$

$$\beta' = [\sigma\alpha-\sigma-1]/[\sigma-(\sigma-1)\alpha]$$

$$\beta'' = [\sigma-(\sigma-1)\alpha]^{-1}$$

$$C = [\alpha a]^{-1}$$

## Appendix II

### Stationarity tests for the variables used in the empirical model

| | Functional Form | D-F t Statistic | Mackinon Cr. t Value |
|---|---|---|---|
| $C^e$ | T,1 | 2.71 | 3.62 |
| Y | T,1 | 3.89 | 3.62 |
| $Y^e$ | T,1 | 6.07 | 3.00 |
| RESY | C,1 | 3.22 | 3.00 |
| G | C,1 | 3.38 | 3.00 |
| $G^e$ | C,1 | 5.27 | 3.00 |
| RESG | N,2 | 2.55 | 1.96* |
| R | C,2 | 2.78 | 3.00 |
| $R^e$ | T,2 | 3.65 | 3.63 |
| RESR | N,2 | 3.05 | 1.95 |
| IM | C,0 | 1.63 | 3.00 |
| $IM^e$ | C,3 | 3.08 | 3.01 |
| RESM | N,2 | 2.28 | 1.96 |
| $I^e$ | C,4 | 3.37 | 3.04 |
| $I^P$ | C,2 | 3.24 | 3.02 |
| Q | T,1 | 3.18 | 3.62* |
| K | C,1 | 3.98 | 3.01 |
| E | T,0 | 2.80 | 3.65 |
| N | T,3 | 2.67 | 3.67 |
| $P^E/P$ | T,2 | 3.24 | 3.66 |
| $P^K/W$ | T,2 | 3.52 | 3.66* |
| W | T,1 | 2.43 | 3.01 |
| TF | T,0 | 3.05 | 3.65 |

Notes: * indicates significance at the 10% level. In the second column, C and T indicate whether a constant or a constant and a trend variable are included and the number of lagged difference terms in the regression. N indicates the exclusion of both C and T. The t statistics in the third and fourth columns are in absolute values. If the t value in the third column is greater than the value in the fourth column the null hypothesis of the existence of a unit root is rejected at the 5% level.

## NOTES

1.   For a random walk consumption function using a constant elasticity utility function, see Raut and Virmani (1989, p. 382).

2.   As in the earlier studies in the literature, we work in log-linear relationships even though there is no a priori reason for selecting this over other functional forms, a point argued by Blinder and Deaton (1985).

3.   This approach has been used in a number of Computable General Equilibrium models for some developing economies (see, for example, Robinson (1989)).

4.   This is also the procedure used by Conway for Turkey (Conway 1987).

5.   Similar findings were reached by Conway (1987) for Turkey.

# 6 Simulation of the model

## 6.1 Introduction

This chapter uses the estimated macroeconomic model of chapter 5 to analyze the quantitative effects of external shocks and government policy variables on Kenya's current account for the period 1974-88. The model allows us to separate the effects of external shocks from the effects of government policy in response to the shocks. As noted in chapter 5, 1973 was the first time since independence that Kenya experienced a major external shock. Therefore, we chose the period after 1973 to analyze the impact of the external shocks to the economy.

The analysis is undertaken using the behavioural equations estimated in chapter 5. The path of the economy is simulated under various assumptions regarding the time paths of the exogenous and government policy variables. For simulation purposes, we used the Micro TSP program version 7.0. This program uses the Gauss Seidel algorithm to compute the values of the endogenous variables.

The rest of this chapter is organized as follows: section 2 sets out the specific equations of the macroeconomic model used for the simulations. Section 3 provides a historical simulation of the economy using the actual values of the exogenous and government policy variables. In section 4, simulation experiments are performed under various assumptions regarding the time paths of the exogenous and government policy variables.

## 6.2 The macroeconomic model

The macroeconomic model used for the simulations is based on the absorption approach to the balance of payments analysis. This approach is useful for our purposes for three main reasons. First, it enables us to express the current account as the difference between total output supply and total expenditure, which then allows us to incorporate the behavioral equations of private agents and the government into the analysis. Second, this approach makes it possible to introduce intertemporal optimization behaviour into the analysis. Recent research in developing countries is increasingly using this type of analysis (see, for example, Haque *et al* 1990). Third, this approach enables us to incorporate the key structural features of the Kenyan economy discussed in chapter 4.

The equations used in the simulation exercise are specified below. Except where indicated, the definitions of the symbols are as given in earlier chapters. All the variables are in natural logarithms except for the following: $Y^G_t$ in equation (6.1) which expresses gross output as the sum of total domestic value added and imported inputs (see chapter 4); variable $A_t$ in equation (6.9) which defines domestic absorption and variable $B_t$ in equation (6.10) which define the current account balance. In equation (6.3), the workers' consumption is expressed as the product of the real wage and labour demand. Capitalist consumption is represented by equation (6.7) and equation (6.8) represents private investment. Equations (6.4), (6.5) and (6.6) represent domestic value added and the demand functions for labour and imported inputs respectively. The current account is expressed as gross output less domestic absorption and imported inputs in equation (6.10).

$$Y^G_t = \exp(Y_t) + \exp(E_t) \qquad (6.1)$$

$$Q_t = \log(Y^G_t) \qquad (6.2)$$

$$C^w_t = \log(N.w)_t \qquad (6.3)$$

$$Y_t = 0.59 + 0.29K_t + 0.82N_t \qquad (6.4)$$

$$N_t = 3.54 + 0.01K_t + 0.89Q_t - 0.55(W/P)_t \qquad (6.5)$$

$$E_t = -2.29 + 1.13Q_t - 0.38(P^E/P)_t - 3.10TF_t \qquad (6.6)$$

$$C^c_t = -5.35 - 0.37C^c_{t-1} + 5.05Y^c_t - 3.36(Y_t - Y^c_t)$$

$$- 2.44G^c_t + 0.55(G_t - G^c_t)$$

$$+ 1.51IM^c_t - 0.19(IM_t - IM^c_t)$$

$$- 8.37R^c_t - 0.99(R_t - R^c_t) \tag{6.7}$$

$$I^p_t = - 25.71 + 2.83Y_t - 1.04I^g_t - 0.87(P^K/W)_t$$

$$- 0.73R_t + 0.64IM_t + K_t \tag{6.8}$$

$$A_t = exp(C^c_t) + exp(C^w_t) + exp(I^p_t) + exp(G_t) \tag{6.9}$$

$$B_t = exp(Q_t) - A_t - exp(E_t) \tag{6.10}$$

All government policy variables are assumed to be predetermined. This is consistent with the conclusion in chapter 4 that the interaction between the government and the private sector in Kenya can best be described as a non-cooperative Stackleberg game where the government is the leader.

## 6.3 Model simulation

The simulation procedure involves a set of experiments which examine the contribution of each external shock being considered in the determination of the current account. In order to analyze the quantitative effects of the external shocks and the government policy variables, it is necessary to have a benchmark with which various scenarios can be compared. The benchmark run is generated under specified assumptions regarding the time paths of the external and government policy variables. It is assumed that the exogenous and government policy variables followed the same trend as in the pre-shock period which in our case is assumed to be 1973 (see chapter 5).

Using the base values of the exogenous and government policy variables, a numerical calibration of the model is undertaken which represents the time path of the economy. This benchmark simulation attempts to answer the following question: how would the economy have behaved in the absence of external shocks and the policy responses that ensued?

To analyze the effect of the external shocks and government policy variables, a dynamic simulation of the model is undertaken where each of the variables is changed from its benchmark value to its actual value. The new values of the endogenous variables including the current account are then compared with their benchmark values. The percentage change in the endogenous variables (calculated as the difference between the benchmark values and the new values) is attributed to the external shock or government policy variable under consideration. The sections which follow describe the various simulations that are undertaken.

### 6.3.1 Historical simulation

Table 6.1 represents the results of the historical simulation of the model. The data represent the percentage change of predicted values of endogenous variables from their actual values. The deviations in the current account were estimated in level form since negative deviations cannot be computed in logarithms. The results show that the historical model fits the data well. Except for private investment and the current account, none of the simulated values exceeds its actual value by more than 12%. The graphical presentation of the results in figure 6.1 supports these findings.

There are several distinctive features that can be observed from table 6.1 and figure 6.1. The deviations from actual values are smaller for the period 1974-1980 than for the period 1981-1988. Except for workers' consumption, the percentage deviations are twice as high for the second period. For the first period (1974-1980), the model tends to undershoot the actual values except for private investment. For the second period, the model tends to overshoot the actual values. Deviations in the current account are relatively smaller for the period 1977-79, reflecting the favourable external position due to the coffee boom during 1976-79 (see chapter 2).

The deviations tend to increase for the years immediately following the negative external shocks, while they decrease following positive external shocks. For example, the deviations increase for years 1974-1975 and 1979-1981. These two respective periods follow the two major oil shocks of 1973 and 1979. A similar pattern can be seen after the coffee boom period of 1976.

The relatively poor performance of the model in the second period can be explained by a number of factors. First, there were major structural shifts in the 1980s reflecting the effects of the second oil crisis and the world recession of 1980-81 which had serious contractionary effects in the economy. The effects of the first oil price shock were partly offset by the favourable coffee boom prices of 1976. Also, the political uncertainties associated with the attempted coup in 1982 partly explain why actual investment was below predicted values in the second period.

## Table 6.1

### Deviation of predicted values of endogenous variables
### from actual values
### (in percentages)

|      | Q    | Y    | N    | E    | C$^c$ | C$^w$ | I$^p$ | B       |
|------|------|------|------|------|------|------|------|---------|
| 1974 | 1.6  | 2.1  | 1.8  | 0.5  | -1.1 | 0.0  | 29.4 | -208.1  |
| 1975 | 2.7  | 2.4  | 2.4  | 5.2  | -0.1 | 0.0  | 31.9 | -224.4  |
| 1976 | 0.8  | 0.1  | -0.7 | 5.0  | 1.6  | 0.0  | 21.6 | -290.2  |
| 1977 | -1.6 | -1.6 | -2.5 | -2.2 | 1.2  | 0.0  | 10.7 | -192.9  |
| 1978 | 0.4  | -0.1 | 0.1  | 3.6  | 0.7  | 0.0  | 17.2 | -135.1  |
| 1979 | -0.1 | -0.2 | -0.4 | 0.6  | -0.5 | 0.0  | 21.0 | -138.0  |
| 1980 | -1.6 | -1.1 | -1.7 | -5.8 | 3.2  | 0.0  | 18.4 | -252.8  |
| 1981 | -2.3 | 2.7  | -3.4 | -0.3 | 1.7  | 0.0  | 10.6 | -377.5  |
| 1982 | 1.2  | 0.8  | 1.2  | 6.2  | 0.5  | 0.0  | 29.9 | -669.9  |
| 1983 | 5.6  | 5.6  | 7.2  | 9.1  | -0.6 | 0.0  | 56.3 | -2309.7 |
| 1984 | 5.4  | 5.6  | 7.1  | 6.9  | -0.6 | 0.0  | 55.8 | -2001.4 |
| 1985 | 6.3  | 6.1  | 7.9  | 11.9 | -1.2 | 0.0  | 61.3 | 3807.4  |
| 1986 | 4.9  | 4.7  | 6.5  | 8.1  | -1.4 | 0.0  | 48.6 | -1625.4 |
| 1987 | 4.3  | 4.2  | 6.0  | 6.8  | -2.1 | -0.0 | 48.1 | -1314.6 |
| 1988 | 3.4  | 3.5  | 5.2  | 4.7  | -2.3 | 0.0  | 41.1 | -449.8  |

Notes: I$^p$ and B represent private investment and the current account balance respectively. All the other variables are as defined in earlier chapters. These definitions are retained throughout this chapter.

## Figure 6.1

## Deviation of predicted values from actual values
of endogenous variables

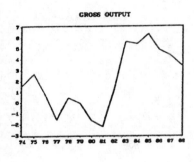

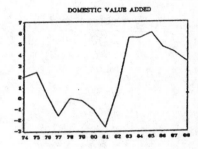

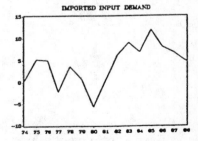

**Figure 6.1 (continued)**

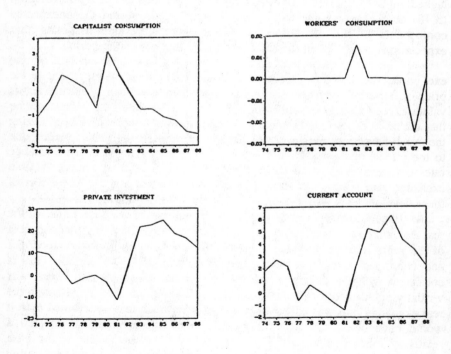

## 6.3.2 Base simulation of the model

The base simulation provides a counterfactual portrayal of the economy based on the assumption that no external shock affected the economy during the period. It is the benchmark against which we measure the impact of external shocks and government policy variables on the endogenous variables of the system. To simulate the counterfactual solution, benchmark (or base values) of the exogenous and government policy variables have to be generated. As in the previous chapter, we assume that these variables continued to follow the same trend as in the pre-shock period. Except for the expected and unexpected components of the consumption function, base values for the exogenous and government policy variables were generated by regressing each variable on its lagged value for the pre-shock period. The regressions are based on equation (5.18) of chapter 5. The base values for the expected and the unexpected components of the consumption function were generated assuming that expectations continued in the same trend as in the pre-shock period.

Figure 6.2 represents the deviations of the base values of the exogenous variables from their actual (historical) values. With regard to the price of imported inputs, the deviations are negative indicating that the actual values exceed their base values for the entire period. The base values assume that the price of imported inputs grew at the slower trend experienced during the pre-1974 period. However, the actual values increased faster, mainly due to the effects of the oil price shocks in 1973 and 1979. Also, the exchange rate was devalued several times after 1974 and a relatively more flexible exchange rate policy was adopted after 1984 (see chapter 2). The effect of these developments was to increase the price of imported inputs.

Except for the 1977-81 period, the deviations of the base values of the real exchange rate from its actual values are negative implying that for most of the years, the real exchange rate would have been highly overvalued if it had continued along the same trend as in the pre-1974 period. This is consistent with the developments in the nominal exchange rate which was virtually unchanged for the latter period, as noted in chapter 2. Although the real exchange rate was still overvalued, it was much less overvalued than it would have been, especially after 1981 when the government adopted a relatively more flexible exchange rate policy. The deviations of the base values of the capacity to import are positive throughout the period indicating that after 1973, the capacity to import declined below what it would have been had conditions remained unchanged from the pre-1974 period.

The base values of government investment are less than their actual (historical) values during 1976-83. This period coincides with the beginning of the coffee boom in 1976. The main explanation for this is the positive effect of the coffee boom on government revenues which contributed to an increase in government investment. In their analysis of the macroeconomic effects of the coffee boom, Bevan, Collier, and Gunning (1993) reach a similar conclusion. They show that the boom led to large investment expenditures which continued beyond the boom period. Total government expenditures exceed their base values throughout the simulation period.

The base values of the real wage exceed their actual values except for 1981, largely reflecting the government's policy of keeping the growth in real wages below the rate of inflation. In chapter 2, we saw that there was a significant fall in real wages after 1982. However, the base values of the relative price of capital ($P^K/W$) were below their actual values for the entire period. The deviations of the tariff rate from its base values largely reflect the variable nature of tariff policy which was mainly driven by the need to raise revenue and to conserve foreign exchange. The base values were derived assuming a relatively stable and more favourable foreign exchange position and thus lower tariffs than the actual outcome after 1974.

Table 6.2 compares the base values of the endogenous variables with the historical values of the model. The deviations are generally smaller for the 1976-1980 and 1977-88 periods except for private investment. Deviations for private investment increased from 10.4 percent in 1974 to 37.5 percent in 1983, and thereafter declined slightly to 33 percent in 1988. The base values for gross output, imported inputs, workers' consumption and private investment exceed their historical values indicating that had conditions continued along the pre-1974 trend, these variables would have been higher. The historical values for capitalist consumption exceed the base values implying that capitalists adjusted by reducing consumption. Domestic value added and the demand for labour do not have major deviations.

The data in table 6.2 show that in the absence of external shocks and the corresponding government policy responses, the current account would have been worse than the scenario indicated by historical data. This is largely explained by the deviations of the base values of private investment and workers' consumption from their historical values. The deviations for these variables averaged 25 and 3.2 percent respectively for the entire period, with respective peaks of 37.5 and 7.3 percent in 1983. This implies that domestic absorption would have been substantially higher, and the current account would have been worse if private investment and workers' consumption had remained at their pre-shock levels.

A similar pattern can be seen from figure 6.3. which is a graphical representation of the percentage deviation of the base values of the endogenous variables from the actual values of the model. Private investment far exceeds actual values, especially for the period after 1980. The corresponding values for the current account show a similar pattern.

The findings of table 6.2 and figure 6.3 suggest that there were significant adjustments in production and total expenditure that helped to reduce the current account from what it would have been had external shocks and government policy variables continued at their pre-1973 levels. The following sections analyze the effects of each of the exogenous variables and government policy variables on private production and expenditure and on the current account.

## Table 6.2

### Deviation of the base values of endogenous variables
### from actual values
### (in percentages)

|      | Q    | Y    | N    | E    | $C^c$ | $C^w$ | $I^p$ | B       |
|------|------|------|------|------|-------|-------|-------|---------|
| 1974 | 1.9  | 0.5  | -0.2 | -0.7 | -0.2  | 1.1   | 10.4  | -51.0   |
| 1975 | 12.6 | 0.9  | 0.4  | 6.2  | -2.3  | 2.5   | 12.9  | -28.9   |
| 1976 | 14.9 | 0.9  | 0.2  | 8.6  | 1.6   | 0.5   | 15.7  | -139.5  |
| 1977 | 8.4  | 0.2  | -0.1 | 6.2  | 0.2   | 0.2   | 13.9  | -114.2  |
| 1978 | 9.1  | 0.3  | 0.5  | 6.7  | -2.9  | 1.2   | 12.5  | -44.3   |
| 1979 | 9.7  | 0.5  | 0.6  | 5.6  | -3.8  | 1.3   | 21.4  | -85.7   |
| 1980 | 7.6  | 0.8  | 0.8  | 1.9  | -2.1  | 1.1   | 23.9  | -165.1  |
| 1981 | 17.8 | 0.7  | 1.1  | 13.5 | -0.8  | 0.8   | 25.8  | -395.5  |
| 1982 | 21.4 | 0.8  | 1.3  | 17.5 | -3.8  | 4.1   | 25.0  | -879.5  |
| 1983 | 21.2 | 1.1  | 1.0  | 13.4 | -4.4  | 7.3   | 37.5  | -1057.2 |
| 1984 | 14.0 | 0.6  | 0.7  | 8.9  | -5.6  | 6.9   | 37.5  | -957.1  |
| 1985 | 12.1 | 0.1  | 0.1  | 11.9 | -5.1  | 6.9   | 36.4  | -1276.1 |
| 1986 | 4.5  | -0.5 | -0.4 | 7.7  | -7.0  | 5.4   | 34.7  | -1159.7 |
| 1987 | 0.8  | -0.9 | -0.7 | 6.0  | -7.8  | 4.7   | 32.0  | -656.4  |
| 1988 | -3.6 | -1.3 | -1.0 | 3.9  | -8.5  | 3.9   | 33.0  | -451.7  |

## Figure 6.2

### Deviation of base values of exogenous variables from their actual values (in percentages)

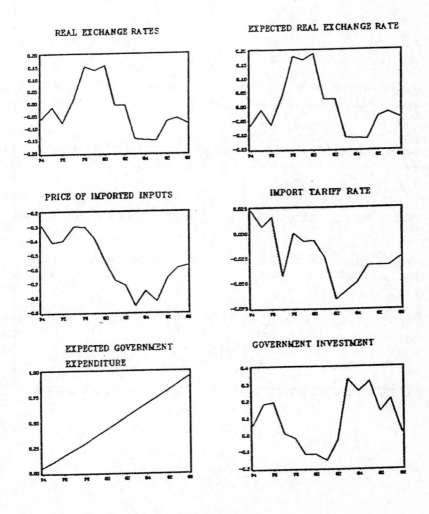

REAL EXCHANGE RATES

EXPECTED REAL EXCHANGE RATE

PRICE OF IMPORTED INPUTS

IMPORT TARIFF RATE

EXPECTED GOVERNMENT EXPENDITURE

GOVERNMENT INVESTMENT

# Figure 6.2 (continued)

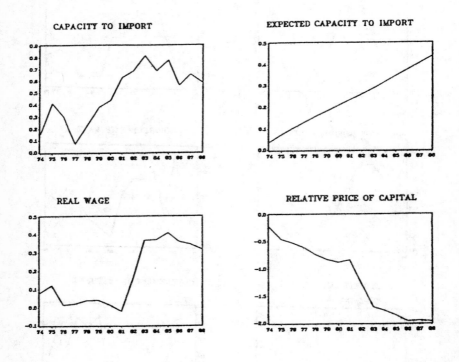

## Figure 6.3

## Deviation of base values of endogenous variables
## from their actual values

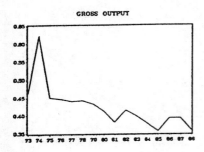

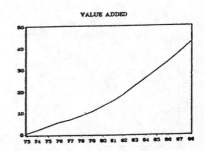

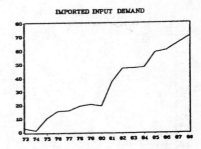

# Figure 6.3 (continued)

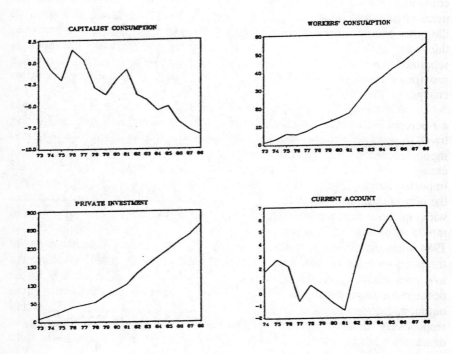

## 6.4 Simulated effects of exogenous shocks and government policy variables

This section presents the effects of changes in the following exogenous and government policy variables: an increase in the price of imported inputs; real exchange rate; government spending; wage policy; and the increase in the relative price of capital.

### 6.4.1 The effect of an increase in the relative price of imported inputs

The effect of an increase in the relative price of imported inputs on private production and expenditure and hence the current account is analyzed by computing the change in the values of the endogenous variables when the price of imported inputs is changed from base to actual values, and when all the other exogenous variables are held unchanged from their base values. In this way, as explained in chapter 4, the effect of the external shock is separated from the effects of the other variables in the system. Table 6.3 provides estimates of the contribution of the imported input price increase to changes in the current account.

Our theoretical prediction represented by equation (6.6) indicates that a 1 percent increase in the price of imported inputs would reduce their demand by 0.38 percent. From figure 6.2, the base values of the price of imported inputs exceeded their historical values between 1981-85, implying that a change in $P^E$ from base to historical values should increase the demand for imported inputs. The effect on the demand for imported inputs for the rest of the period should be negative. The results reported in table 6.3 are consistent with our theoretical prediction since the deviations of the demand for imported inputs from their base values are positive for the period 1981-85 except for 1984 when the deviation was negative and relatively small. Also, the effect of the price increase on the demand for imported inputs is small reflecting the low own elasticity of the demand for imported inputs. The decline in the demand for imported inputs was largely responsible for the declines in gross output and domestic value added, which averaged about 12.2 and 2.2 percent respectively for the whole period. This had an indirect effect of reducing the demand for labour and thus workers' consumption, as can be seen in the third and fifth columns of table 6.3.

The increase in the price of imported inputs also had an indirect effect on private expenditure. Total consumption expenditure declined throughout the period and by higher magnitudes in the 1980s. The decline in private consumption expenditure was largely due to the decline in workers' consumption which was substantially larger than the decline in capitalist

119

consumption. One explanation for this finding is that capitalists have relatively easy access to credit and therefore are able to smooth their consumption over time through borrowing.

The effect of an increase in the relative price of imported inputs on private investment is not consistent with our theoretical prediction. From table 6.3, the deviations of private investment from the base values are positive, indicating that private investment would have increased following the increase in the price of imported inputs. This suggests that there were other factors that influenced private investment that are not captured by our model. According to Bevan, Collier, and Gunning (1993), the Kenyan government operated a wide-ranging control regime established in the late 1960s, which had a strong constraining effect on private sector behaviour particularly in response to external shocks. The control regime included exchange and import controls, and interest, wage, and price controls. The authors show that private agents saved much of the windfall associated with the coffee boom of 1976-79. However, the control regime limited private sector responses to inefficient investment in the nontraded sector, and especially in construction. During the same period, there was a temporary relaxation of import controls which led to excess accumulation of imports in anticipation of reintroduction of the controls in the future. Bevan *et al* note that the construction boom continued well beyond the coffee boom period. These findings are consistent with the positive deviations of private investment and the demand for imported inputs observed in our study.

The above result is nevertheless consistent with theoretical models that integrate optimization behaviour with structural features of developing countries (see, for example, Ostry 1988). These models predict that when the importance of imported inputs is taken into account, the effect of an external shock such as an increase in the price of imported inputs is indeterminate. The overall impact depends on the relative effects on domestic production and absorption. In the case of Kenya, the overall effect was to worsen the current account. Comparing the actual current account balance with what it would have been in the absence of the external shock, there were large deviations for the whole period except during 1976-78 and 1981-83. The change in the tariff rate from base to actual values, as shown in table 6.4, has a similar effect to the change in the price of imported inputs.

## Table 6.3

**The effect of a change in $P^E$ from base
to actual values
(in percentages)**

|      | Q     | Y    | N    | E    | $C^c$ | $C^w$ | $I^p$ | B      |
|------|-------|------|------|------|------|------|------|--------|
| 1974 | -16.9 | -1.9 | -2.9 | -6.5 | -0.2 | -4.4 | -0.3 | -285.8 |
| 1975 | -9.5  | -1.5 | -2.5 | -1.1 | -2.3 | -6.1 | 2.3  | -111.1 |
| 1976 | -5.9  | -1.3 | -2.4 | -1.7 | -1.6 | -7.5 | 6.2  | -45.4  |
| 1977 | -7.7  | -1.5 | -2.2 | -0.9 | -0.2 | -8.7 | 6.4  | -57.1  |
| 1978 | -9.3  | -1.8 | -1.9 | -1.0 | -3.0 | -10.7 | 3.8 | -65.4  |
| 1979 | -12.9 | -2.0 | -2.4 | -1.5 | -3.8 | -12.8 | 10.1 | -110.3 |
| 1980 | -17.5 | -1.9 | -2.6 | -6.5 | -2.1 | -15.1 | 12.0 | -246.5 |
| 1981 | -12.0 | -2.3 | -2.7 | 2.6  | -0.8 | -17.5 | 13.2 | -82.7  |
| 1982 | -9.8  | -2.2 | -2.5 | 6.0  | -3.8 | -19.7 | 21.8 | -57.9  |
| 1983 | -12.0 | -2.1 | -3.1 | 0.9  | -4.4 | -22.4 | 23.7 | -92.8  |
| 1984 | -13.0 | -2.0 | -2.7 | -1.4 | -5.6 | -24.6 | 26.3 | -89.7  |
| 1985 | -16.2 | -2.7 | -3.6 | 0.3  | -5.2 | -27.5 | 24.4 | -206.9 |
| 1986 | -18.9 | -2.9 | -3.5 | -1.4 | -7.0 | -29.8 | 24.8 | -227.6 |
| 1987 | -20.0 | -3.1 | -3.6 | -2.2 | -7.8 | -32.4 | 22.5 | -377.4 |
| 1988 | -23.3 | -3.5 | -3.8 | -4.0 | -8.5 | -35.0 | 23.5 | -583.1 |

## Table 6.4

## The effect of a change in tariff policy (TF)
## from base to actual values
## (in percentages)

|      | Q     | Y    | N    | E    | C<sup>c</sup> | C<sup>w</sup> | I<sup>p</sup> | B     |
|------|-------|------|------|------|------|------|------|-------|
| 1974 | 8.7   | 0.8  | 1.1  | 2.8  | 0.0  | 1.2  | 3.0  | 10.1  |
| 1975 | 2.3   | 0.2  | 0.3  | 0.8  | 0.0  | 0.3  | 0.8  | 13.5  |
| 1976 | 6.3   | 0.6  | 0.8  | 2.0  | 0.0  | 0.9  | 2.1  | 19.7  |
| 1977 | -12.8 | -1.4 | -1.8 | -4.8 | 0.0  | -2.0 | -4.6 | -4.0  |
| 1978 | -10.1 | 0.0  | 0.0  | 0.0  | 0.0  | 0.0  | 0.0  | 4.0   |
| 1979 | -2.5  | -0.2 | -0.3 | -0.9 | 0.0  | -0.4 | -0.8 | -8.5  |
| 1980 | -2.6  | -0.3 | -0.3 | -0.9 | 0.0  | -0.4 | -0.8 | -6.4  |
| 1981 | -7.6  | -0.8 | -1.0 | -2.7 | 0.0  | -1.1 | -2.4 | -8.2  |
| 1982 | -17.9 | -1.9 | -2.5 | -6.9 | 0.0  | -2.7 | -5.8 | -16.2 |
| 1983 | -16.3 | -1.7 | -2.2 | -6.1 | 0.0  | -2.5 | -5.2 | -9.3  |
| 1984 | -14.2 | -1.5 | -1.9 | -5.2 | 0.0  | -2.1 | -4.5 | -9.3  |
| 1985 | -9.9  | -1.0 | -1.3 | -3.5 | 0.0  | -1.4 | -3.0 | -5.3  |
| 1986 | -9.8  | -1.0 | -1.3 | -3.5 | 0.0  | -1.4 | -3.0 | -1.5  |
| 1987 | -9.7  | -1.0 | -1.3 | -3.4 | 0.0  | -1.4 | -3.0 | -3.0  |
| 1988 | -7.3  | -0.7 | -0.9 | -2.5 | 0.0  | -1.0 | -2.2 | -0.1  |

As predicted in the theoretical model in chapter 4, the contractionary effect of the increase in the price of imported inputs and the resulting increase in unemployment is not in the best interest of the government. We noted that one of the main objectives of the government is to maintain reasonable employment levels. Faced with this contractionary effect, the model predicted that the government would react by undertaking policies to maintain employment and the level of output. This could be an increase in government spending or a revaluation of the exchange rate or both. The next subsection examines the effect of a change in the real exchange rate.

### 6.4.2 Real exchange rate appreciation

We mentioned in chapter 2 that the government did not pursue an active exchange rate policy until 1984 when a relatively more flexible policy was adopted. Therefore, the change in the real exchange rate is largely explained by changes in the price level. Changes in the price level in Kenya are explained by two main factors: imported inflation, and increases in money supply arising from domestic credit creation. Lending to the government is one of the main causes of the increase in domestic credit (Killick 1984). It is, therefore, reasonable to conclude that the major cause of inflation in Kenya was increases in money supply, mainly due to government borrowing. In fact, the periods of inflation mainly coincided with periods of domestic credit expansion. Therefore, the real exchange rate appreciation was caused by inflation, mainly associated with expansionary fiscal and monetary policies. The decline in the effect of the real exchange rate on consumption in the second period can be explained by the fact that the government introduced a more flexible exchange rate policy during the second period.

Table 6.5 shows that the effect of a change in the real exchange rate from base to actual values was a relatively small reduction in capitalist consumption, with similar reduction in private investment for most of the period. There was a modest increase in private investment during 1977-80. The effect on the other endogenous variables was insignificant. The effect of changing the real exchange rate from base to actual values on capitalist consumption is consistent with the predictions of our model, as indicated by equation (6.7). However, the behaviour of private investment partially deviates from the prediction of equation (6.8) because it should have declined during 1976-80 instead of the observed increase. This apparent contradiction is explained in section 6.4.1 above and is primarily due to the behaviour of private investment under the control regime that prevailed during the coffee boom period of 1976-79.

**Table 6.5**

**The effect of a change in the real exchange rate
from base to actual values
(in percentages)**

|      | Q   | Y   | N   | E   | C$^c$ | C$^w$ | I$^p$ | B     |
|------|-----|-----|-----|-----|-------|-------|-------|-------|
| 1974 | 0.0 | 0.0 | 0.0 | 0.0 | -2.1  | 0.0   | -0.8  | -26.9 |
| 1975 | 0.0 | 0.0 | 0.0 | 0.0 | -1.6  | 0.0   | -0.2  | -18.1 |
| 1976 | 0.0 | 0.0 | 0.0 | 0.0 | -3.7  | 0.0   | -1.0  | -40.9 |
| 1977 | 0.0 | 0.0 | 0.0 | 0.0 | -2.2  | 0.0   | 0.2   | -15.9 |
| 1978 | 0.0 | 0.0 | 0.0 | 0.0 | -1.1  | 0.0   | 1.8   | -5.2  |
| 1979 | 0.0 | 0.0 | 0.0 | 0.0 | -2.1  | 0.0   | 1.5   | -0.1  |
| 1980 | 0.0 | 0.0 | 0.0 | 0.0 | -1.6  | 0.0   | 1.7   | -6.0  |
| 1981 | 0.0 | 0.0 | 0.0 | 0.0 | -4.5  | 0.0   | -0.1  | -20.0 |
| 1982 | 0.0 | 0.0 | 0.0 | 0.0 | -3.5  | 0.0   | -0.1  | -15.5 |
| 1983 | 0.0 | 0.0 | 0.0 | 0.0 | -6.1  | 0.0   | 1.5   | -37.3 |
| 1984 | 0.0 | 0.0 | 0.0 | 0.0 | -5.3  | 0.0   | -1.6  | -33.5 |
| 1985 | 0.0 | 0.0 | 0.0 | 0.0 | -5.7  | 0.0   | -1.6  | -37.7 |
| 1986 | 0.0 | 0.0 | 0.0 | 0.0 | -4.5  | 0.0   | -0.8  | -25.0 |
| 1987 | 0.0 | 0.0 | 0.0 | 0.0 | -4.9  | 0.0   | -0.6  | -25.0 |
| 1988 | 0.0 | 0.0 | 0.0 | 0.0 | -5.2  | 0.0   | -0.9  | -25.5 |

Theoretically, the overall effect of a change in the real exchange rate from base to actual values should have been to improve the current account. However, our result shows that the current account worsened. A possible explanation for this anomaly is that there were other factors at play that influenced the current account. In chapter 2, we saw that other factors which influence the current account in Kenya and in other small open developing economies include the relatively large outflows of factor income on profits, dividends and interest. The effects of these outflows become more important since the effects of the real exchange rate are relatively small.

### 6.4.3 Government expenditures and the capacity to import

Our theoretical model predicts that an increase in government spending would increase capitalist consumption (equation (6.7)) while an increase in government investment crowds out private investment (equation (6.8)). The capacity to import has a positive effect on both capitalist consumption and private investment.

The effect of changing government spending from base to actual values is reported in table 6.6. The effect on capitalist consumption was positive and reasonably high (averaging about 50 percent) while the effect on private investment was low and mixed. The effect on private investment was negative for the period 1978-82, probably due to the strong crowding effect of high government expenditure during the coffee boom. Reflecting this, the current account improved during 1974-82, and worsened thereafter. As indicated in table 6.7, government investment alone had a similar effect on private investment to that of total government spending. As noted in section 6.3.2 above, the capacity to import was lower than what it would have been if the pre-1974 conditions had prevailed throughout the study period. Substituting the base for the actual values of the capacity to import reduced capitalist consumption and private investment expenditures, as shown in table 6.8. Consequently the current account worsened.

## Table 6.6

### The effect of a change in government spending
### from base to actual values
### (in percentages)

|      | Q   | Y   | N   | E   | $C^c$ | $C^w$ | $I^p$ | B     |
| ---- | --- | --- | --- | --- | ----- | ----- | ----- | ----- |
| 1974 | 0.0 | 0.0 | 0.0 | 0.0 | 16.7  | 0.0   | 1.1   | -8.1  |
| 1975 | 0.0 | 0.0 | 0.0 | 0.0 | 6.7   | 0.0   | 3.3   | -39.6 |
| 1976 | 0.0 | 0.0 | 0.0 | 0.0 | 19.7  | 0.0   | 3.4   | -44.1 |
| 1977 | 0.0 | 0.0 | 0.0 | 0.0 | 17.8  | 0.0   | 0.1   | -13.4 |
| 1978 | 0.0 | 0.0 | 0.0 | 0.0 | 18.0  | 0.0   | -0.3  | -93.4 |
| 1979 | 0.0 | 0.0 | 0.0 | 0.0 | 24.9  | 0.0   | -1.9  | -75.0 |
| 1980 | 0.0 | 0.0 | 0.0 | 0.0 | 25.5  | 0.0   | -1.9  | -32.4 |
| 1981 | 0.0 | 0.0 | 0.0 | 0.0 | 50.6  | 0.0   | -2.4  | -72.0 |
| 1982 | 0.0 | 0.0 | 0.0 | 0.0 | 42.6  | 0.0   | -0.4  | -3.8  |
| 1983 | 0.0 | 0.0 | 0.0 | 0.0 | 97.3  | 0.0   | 4.9   | 209.0 |
| 1984 | 0.0 | 0.0 | 0.0 | 0.0 | 81.1  | 0.0   | 3.8   | 136.1 |
| 1985 | 0.0 | 0.0 | 0.0 | 0.0 | 93.2  | 0.0   | 4.8   | 229.9 |
| 1986 | 0.0 | 0.0 | 0.0 | 0.0 | 71.6  | 0.0   | 2.1   | 82.1  |
| 1987 | 0.0 | 0.0 | 0.0 | 0.0 | 81.2  | 0.0   | 3.2   | 121.1 |
| 1988 | 0.0 | 0.0 | 0.0 | 0.0 | 97.5  | 0.0   | 0.1   | 11.5  |

## Table 6.7

## The effect of a change in government investment from base to actual values (in percentages)

|      | Q   | Y   | N   | E   | $C^c$ | $C^w$ | $I^p$ | B     |
|------|-----|-----|-----|-----|-----|-----|------|-------|
| 1974 | 0.0 | 0.0 | 0.0 | 0.0 | 0.0 | 0.0 | 1.1  | 6.1   |
| 1975 | 0.0 | 0.0 | 0.0 | 0.0 | 0.0 | 0.0 | 3.4  | -20.5 |
| 1976 | 0.0 | 0.0 | 0.0 | 0.0 | 0.0 | 0.0 | 3.5  | -21.4 |
| 1977 | 0.0 | 0.0 | 0.0 | 0.0 | 0.0 | 0.0 | 0.1  | -0.8  |
| 1978 | 0.0 | 0.0 | 0.0 | 0.0 | 0.0 | 0.0 | -0.3 | 2.3   |
| 1979 | 0.0 | 0.0 | 0.0 | 0.0 | 0.0 | 0.0 | -1.9 | 14.8  |
| 1980 | 0.0 | 0.0 | 0.0 | 0.0 | 0.0 | 0.0 | -1.9 | 15.9  |
| 1981 | 0.0 | 0.0 | 0.0 | 0.0 | 0.0 | 0.0 | -2.4 | 22.5  |
| 1982 | 0.0 | 0.0 | 0.0 | 0.0 | 0.0 | 0.0 | -0.4 | 3.9   |
| 1983 | 0.0 | 0.0 | 0.0 | 0.0 | 0.0 | 0.0 | -4.9 | -36.0 |
| 1984 | 0.0 | 0.0 | 0.0 | 0.0 | 0.0 | 0.0 | 3.8  | -28.3 |
| 1985 | 0.0 | 0.0 | 0.0 | 0.0 | 0.0 | 0.0 | 4.7  | -35.1 |
| 1986 | 0.0 | 0.0 | 0.0 | 0.0 | 0.0 | 0.0 | 2.2  | -16.5 |
| 1987 | 0.0 | 0.0 | 0.0 | 0.0 | 0.0 | 0.0 | 3.1  | -24.4 |
| 1988 | 0.0 | 0.0 | 0.0 | 0.0 | 0.0 | 0.0 | 0.1  | -0.1  |

## Table 6.8

### The effect of a change in the capacity to import
### from base to actual values
### (in percentages)

| | Q | Y | N | E | $C^c$ | $C^w$ | $I^p$ | B |
|------|-----|-----|-----|-----|------|-----|------|------|
| 1974 | 0.0 | 0.0 | 0.0 | 0.0 | -0.9 | 0.0 | -1.7 | 11.9 |
| 1975 | 0.0 | 0.0 | 0.0 | 0.0 | -0.7 | 0.0 | -4.4 | 22.5 |
| 1976 | 0.0 | 0.0 | 0.0 | 0.0 | -1.9 | 0.0 | -3.2 | 23.7 |
| 1977 | 0.0 | 0.0 | 0.0 | 0.0 | -2.9 | 0.0 | -0.7 | 25.4 |
| 1978 | 0.0 | 0.0 | 0.0 | 0.0 | -2.6 | 0.0 | -2.4 | 35.7 |
| 1979 | 0.0 | 0.0 | 0.0 | 0.0 | -2.9 | 0.0 | -3.7 | 45.3 |
| 1980 | 0.0 | 0.0 | 0.0 | 0.0 | -3.2 | 0.0 | -4.2 | 46.9 |
| 1981 | 0.0 | 0.0 | 0.0 | 0.0 | -3.1 | 0.0 | -5.9 | 53.0 |
| 1982 | 0.0 | 0.0 | 0.0 | 0.0 | -3.6 | 0.0 | -6.3 | 53.9 |
| 1983 | 0.0 | 0.0 | 0.0 | 0.0 | -3.7 | 0.0 | -7.4 | 56.5 |
| 1984 | 0.0 | 0.0 | 0.0 | 0.0 | -4.8 | 0.0 | -6.2 | 53.6 |
| 1985 | 0.0 | 0.0 | 0.0 | 0.0 | -4.8 | 0.0 | -7.1 | 53.1 |
| 1986 | 0.0 | 0.0 | 0.0 | 0.0 | -6.1 | 0.0 | -5.1 | 46.6 |
| 1987 | 0.0 | 0.0 | 0.0 | 0.0 | -6.1 | 0.0 | -5.9 | 49.7 |
| 1988 | 0.0 | 0.0 | 0.0 | 0.0 | -7.0 | 0.0 | -5.2 | 50.5 |

## Table 6.9

### The effect of a change in wage policy
### from base to actual values
### (in percentages)

|      | Q     | Y    | N    | E    | $C^c$ | $C^w$ | $I^p$ | B     |
|------|-------|------|------|------|-------|-------|-------|-------|
| 1974 | 15.8  | 2.0  | 2.6  | 2.8  | -2.1  | 1.6   | 7.1   | -50.0 |
| 1975 | 25.7  | 3.1  | 4.0  | 4.4  | -1.6  | 2.5   | 10.7  | -57.4 |
| 1976 | 2.4   | 0.3  | 0.4  | 0.5  | -3.7  | 0.3   | 1.1   | -2.1  |
| 1977 | 3.1   | 0.4  | 0.6  | 0.6  | -2.2  | 0.3   | 1.4   | -14.0 |
| 1978 | 6.9   | 0.9  | 1.2  | 1.3  | -1.1  | 0.7   | 3.0   | -26.0 |
| 1979 | 7.2   | 0.9  | 1.2  | 1.3  | -2.1  | 0.7   | 2.9   | -26.2 |
| 1980 | 1.6   | 0.2  | 0.3  | 0.3  | -1.6  | 0.1   | 0.7   | -8.6  |
| 1981 | -3.7  | -0.5 | -0.6 | -0.7 | -4.5  | -0.4  | -1.6  | -21.3 |
| 1982 | 35.7  | 3.9  | 5.1  | 5.5  | -3.5  | 3.1   | 12.1  | -34.5 |
| 1983 | 99.9  | 8.8  | 11.5 | 12.5 | -6.1  | 7.0   | 27.0  | -30.5 |
| 1984 | 100.5 | 8.8  | 11.6 | 12.5 | -5.3  | 7.0   | 27.1  | -30.5 |
| 1985 | 116.1 | 9.8  | 12.8 | 13.9 | -5.7  | 7.8   | 30.0  | -28.2 |
| 1986 | 96.6  | 8.6  | 11.2 | 12.2 | -4.5  | 6.8   | 26.3  | -30.2 |
| 1987 | 91.4  | 8.2  | 10.7 | 11.7 | -4.9  | 6.5   | 25.1  | -29.8 |
| 1988 | 80.9  | 7.5  | 9.8  | 10.7 | -5.2  | 5.9   | 22.8  | -30.1 |

## Table 6.10

### The effect of a change in $(P^K/W)$
### from base to actual values
### (in percentages)

|      | Q   | Y   | N   | E   | $C^c$ | $C^w$ | $I^p$ | B      |
|------|-----|-----|-----|-----|-----|-----|-------|--------|
| 1974 | 0.0 | 0.0 | 0.0 | 0.0 | 0.0 | 0.0 | -3.4  | 54.7   |
| 1975 | 0.0 | 0.0 | 0.0 | 0.0 | 0.0 | 0.0 | -6.1  | 260.8  |
| 1976 | 0.0 | 0.0 | 0.0 | 0.0 | 0.0 | 0.0 | -6.5  | -135.8 |
| 1977 | 0.0 | 0.0 | 0.0 | 0.0 | 0.0 | 0.0 | -6.9  | -77.8  |
| 1978 | 0.0 | 0.0 | 0.0 | 0.0 | 0.0 | 0.0 | -7.6  | -61.5  |
| 1979 | 0.0 | 0.0 | 0.0 | 0.0 | 0.0 | 0.0 | -7.8  | -51.3  |
| 1980 | 0.0 | 0.0 | 0.0 | 0.0 | 0.0 | 0.0 | -7.7  | -42.5  |
| 1981 | 0.0 | 0.0 | 0.0 | 0.0 | 0.0 | 0.0 | -6.7  | -32.1  |
| 1982 | 0.0 | 0.0 | 0.0 | 0.0 | 0.0 | 0.0 | -9.4  | -38.7  |
| 1983 | 0.0 | 0.0 | 0.0 | 0.0 | 0.0 | 0.0 | -11.5 | -41.9  |
| 1984 | 0.0 | 0.0 | 0.0 | 0.0 | 0.0 | 0.0 | -11.0 | -36.1  |
| 1985 | 0.0 | 0.0 | 0.0 | 0.0 | 0.0 | 0.0 | -10.6 | -31.8  |
| 1986 | 0.0 | 0.0 | 0.0 | 0.0 | 0.0 | 0.0 | -10.4 | -28.6  |
| 1987 | 0.0 | 0.0 | 0.0 | 0.0 | 0.0 | 0.0 | -9.5  | -24.4  |
| 1988 | 0.0 | 0.0 | 0.0 | 0.0 | 0.0 | 0.0 | -8.8  | -21.3  |

## 6.4.4 *Wage policy and the relative price of capital*

The effects of the wage policy in Kenya are reported in table 6.9. This table shows that the real wage policy did not have any significant effect until the early 1980s. Chapter 2 had pointed out that real wages did not fall until after 1983 when the government undertook serious structural adjustment measures. After 1983, real wages were below what they could have been had the policies remained at their pre-1974 levels.

The effects of the fall in real wages was to increase output, employment and the demand for both labour and capital in the second period. Private consumption declined but workers' consumption increased. The increase in workers' consumption is largely explained by the increase in the demand for labour and thus in employment as real wages fell. The overall effect on the current account was positive. Private investment also increased. These results are consistent with the predictions of the estimated model represented by equations (6.3) and (6.5).

The fall in real wages contributed to the decline in the price of capital relative to the price of labour. Consequently, private investment increased substantially in the second half as shown in table 6.6. During the first half, the price of capital relative to labour was high. This had a negative effect on private investment. This result shows that reducing the price of capital stimulated investment.

## Conclusions

The conclusions derived from the simulation experiments in this chapter are as follows:

i. Exogenous shocks which increased the cost of imported inputs had a contractionary effect on output supply. The effects of the shocks were to reduce the demand for imported inputs and labour, and to reduce the supply of output.

ii. The above contractionary effect is consistent with the theoretical predictions of the neoclassical production theory. It shows that private producers behave in an optimizing manner and would respond to negative external shocks by reducing production.

iii. Exogenous shocks also influenced private expenditures on consumption and investment.

iv. The net effect of the external shocks which were considered was to improve the current account. This means that, in the absence of government intervention, private producers adjusted their behaviour in a manner which improved the current account. Also, the effects were stronger in the 1980s than in the 1970s.

v. The effect of government policies over the period was varied. In general, expansive government spending and a less flexible exchange rate policy stimulated private spending (especially consumption) and consequently had a large and negative effect on the current account.

vi. Government wage policy had a significant effect on employment and output supply, consistent with the theoretical model. This was much clearer in the period after 1980 when the government allowed real wages to fall substantially.

# 7 Summary and conclusions

This book has developed a macroeconomic model to analyze the effects of external shocks - including both government policy and private responses to them - on the current account of the balance of payments in Kenya for the period 1973-1988.

Chapter 2 showed that external shocks such as the worsening of the terms of trade, the reduced demand for exports and high world interest rates had a major influence on the current account in Kenya since the early 1970s. The terms of trade shocks were particularly important during the oil price shocks of 1973 and 1979, and during the commodity booms of 1977 and 1986. In addition, the recession and high interest rates in the world economy during the early 1980s contributed to low export earnings and a substantial increase in outflows. In response to such shocks, the government undertook policy measures which influenced the current account directly through their influence on absorption, and indirectly through their influence on private investment and saving.

Most of the empirical literature on developing economies uses a broadly similar approach in which the contribution of external shocks and government policy responses are separately analyzed by reference to a situation in which the shocks are assumed not to have occurred. While these studies are important, they are based on a rather simple accounting procedure that gives little idea of the interrelationships within the economy. In addition, the influence of the government policy responses on private savings and investment behaviour is often ignored.

To establish the full effects of the external shocks on the current account, a complete model is required in which the responses of both the government and the private sector are derived from an optimizing framework that incorporates all the relevant interrelationships. Although studies of this nature are available for the developed economies, they have rarely been attempted for developing economies. One explanation for this omission is the argument advanced by the structuralist theorists that neoclassical optimizing models are not applicable to developing economies in which the structural rigidities and supply bottlenecks inhibit the smooth functioning of markets. By comparison, this book contends that even in developing economies, economic agents do try to make adjustments and that the neoclassical models can still be used to analyze economic issues in developing countries, particularly if they are modified to take into account the influence of the relevant rigidities. This book has presented a macroeconomic model which incorporates both the neoclassical and the main structural features of the Kenyan economy to analyze the interactions between the government and private sector responses to external shocks and their effect on the current account. The responses of both agents are derived from a choice theoretic framework which enables us to explicitly analyze the influence of government policy on private sector saving, investment and the current account.

The main specific objective of this book was to develop a macroeconomic model to derive the direct and the indirect effects of the external shocks on the current account. The direct effects are due to the effects of the policies on domestic absorption and the indirect effects are a result of the influence of government policy on private production and spending behaviour (through saving and investment). The influence of government policies on private sector behaviour was captured in a game theoretic framework and was empirically tested for Kenya.

A second specific objective of this book was to test empirically whether economic agents in Kenya behave in a forward looking manner. This issue is increasingly becoming important in the literature on developing economies. We also tested whether the Kenyan economy has the necessary flexibility to enable an optimal response by private producers to external shocks. The structuralist approach argues that developing countries do not have enough flexibility to respond to external shocks. This question is important in determining how developing countries respond to external shocks.

A third objective of the book was to test the nature of the interaction between the government and private agents and whether this can be analyzed in a game theoretic framework. Previous studies in the literature had assumed that government behaviour is independent of private sector behaviour. This assumption needs to be tested empirically, as we have done.

The empirical answers to the above issues are provided for Kenya in chapters 5 and 6 above. Their findings are:

i) Governmental policy responses to external shocks did have, as hypothesized, both direct and indirect effects on the current account. The direct influence of government policy on the private sector did not always worsen the current account. However, government spending tended to increase consumption and reduce private investment, to which the private sector responded. The net effect worsened the current account.

ii) The largest impact of the adjustment policies was on private investment and workers' consumption. Workers' consumption declined substantially after 1980, mainly because of a reduction in real wages. Capitalist consumption was not affected by the same magnitude.

iii) Private producers responded to external shocks by adjusting their demand for imported inputs. Therefore, our findings do not support the structuralist assumption that there is no flexibility in production. Moreover, increases in the prices of imported inputs did not worsen the current account to the extent implied by a rigid economic structure. We found that private agents responded in a manner that tended to lessen the adverse impact of increases in the price of the imported inputs on the current account. Similar conclusions applied to the effects of exchange rate changes.

iv) The assumption of forward looking behaviour was not conclusive in the Kenyan case. Both expected and unexpected components of the explanatory variables were statistically significant. This could be due to a number of explanations as specified in chapter 5. These results are similar to those in many studies for the developing and the developed economies.

v. The test for the interaction between the government and the private sector indicated a Stackleberg game structure where the government is the leader.

One of the conclusions from the above findings is that the indirect effect of government policies on private sector behaviour is crucial in determining the overall effect of external shocks on the current account. Although external shocks were found to be contractionary, the *persistence* of current account deficits can be largely explained by government policies. The implication of our findings for policy formulation is that the government must take into account the influence of its policies on private sector behaviour, because the latter's reaction has consequences for the overall macroeconomic performance of the economy.

# Data sources and definitions

The data used in this book have been taken from Vandermortelle (1985); Kenya Government, *Statistical Abstracts*, various years, Nairobi: Government Printer; IMF, *International Financial Statistics*, Washington: The IMF; World Bank, *World Tables*, Washington: The World Bank.

Unless otherwise indicated, the reported data are in Kenya pounds (K$) million, with twenty Kenya shillings to the Kenya £.

The definitions of the main symbols used in this book are:

Q Gross Output, defined as Domestic Value Added plus Imported Inputs.

Y Domestic Value Added, defined as Gross Domestic Product at Factor Cost.

A Domestic Absorption.

K Total Capital Stock. Its series is generated using the following formula: $K_{t+1} = (1-\delta)K_t + I_t$ . The sectoral rates of depreciation ($\delta$) and definitions are explained in Vandermortelle (1985).

E Total Imported Inputs by the private sector. E excludes Imported Capital Equipment.

N Total Formal Sector Employment.

P Domestic Price Level.

$P^E$ Price of Imported Inputs. Estimated by the Import Price Index, 1976=100.

W Nominal Wage, calculated as Total Wage Earnings divided by Total Wage Employment.

w Real Wage, defined as nominal wage divided by the Consumer Price Index.

$\omega$ Wealth.

M       Money Stock.

X       Exports.

IM      Imports.

B       Balance of Payments on Current Account.

$\kappa$       Balance of Payments on Capital Account.

N       Net Foreign Assets.

$C^c$      Capitalist Consumption, estimated by Total Private Consumption less Workers' Consumption.

$C^w$      Workers' Consumption estimated as Total Wage Earnings.

G       Total Government Expenditures.

$I^g$      Government Investment.

$I^p$      Private Investment.

R       Real Exchange Rate, defined as $R = (NR.USCPI)/CPI$, where NR is the Nominal Exchange Rate, USCPI is the United States Consumer Price Index (used a proxy for the world price level) and CPI is the Kenyan Consumer Price Index.

CPI     Consumer Price Index for Kenya.

$P*^E$     Foreign Price of Imported Inputs.

$P^K$      Price of Capital, estimated by the Capital Stock Deflator.

$P*^K$     Foreign Price of Capital, obtained by dividing the domestic price of capital by the exchange rate between the US dollar (representing the 'world currency') and the Kenya Shilling.

# Bibliography

Abel, Andrew. "Consumption and Investment". In Friedman and Hahn (1990).

----------------. "Dynamic Effects of Permanent and Temporary Tax Policies in a q Model of Investment". *Journal of Monetary Economics* 9 (May 1982): 353-73.

----------------. *Investment and the Value of Capital*. New York: Garland, 1979.

Agenor, Pierre-Richard. "Output, Devaluation, and the Real Exchange Rate in Developing Countries". *Weltwirtschaftliches* 127 (1991): 18-41.

Alexander, Sidney. "Effects of Devaluation on the Trade Balance". *International Monetary Fund Staff Papers* 2 (April 1952): 263-78.

Ando, Albert, and Modigliani, Franco. "The Life Cycle Hypothesis of Saving: Aggregate Implications and Tests". *American Economic Review* 53 (March 1963): 55-84.

Arrow, Kenneth J.; Chenery, Hollis B.; Minhas, Bagisha S.; and Solow, Robert M. "Capital Labor Substitution and Economic Efficiency". *Review of Economics and Statistics* 43 (August 1961): 225-50.

Balassa, Bela. *Comparative Advantage, Trade Policy, and Economic*

*Development*. New York: New York University Press, 1989.

----------------. "Adjustment Policies in Developing Countries: A Reassessment". *World Development* 12 (September 1984): 955-72.

----------------. "Structural Adjustment Policies in Developing Countries". *World Development* 10 (January 1982): 23-38.

----------------. "Adjustment to External Shocks in Developing Economies". *Staff Working Paper* no. 472. Washington D.C.: The World Bank, July 1981.

----------------. "The Process of Industrial Development Under Alternative Development Strategies". *Staff Working Paper* no. 438. Washington, D.C.: The World Bank, 1980b.

----------------. "Newly Industrialized Countries after the Oil Crisis". *Staff Working Paper* no. 437. Washington, D.C.: The World Bank, October 1980a.

Balassa, Bela, and McCarthy, Desmond. "Adjustment Policies in Developing Countries 1979-82". *Staff Working Paper* no. 675. Washington, D.C.: The World Bank, April 1984.

Barbara, Grosh. "Parastatal-Led Development: The Financial Sector in Kenya: 1971-1987". *African Development Review* 2 (December 1987): 27-48.

Barbone, Luca, and Rivera-Batiz, Francisco. "Foreign Capital and the Contractionary Impact of Currency Devaluation, with an Application to Jamaica". *Journal of Development Economics* 26 (January 1987): 1-15.

Basar, Tamar. *Dynamic Games and Applications in Economics*. Berlin: Springer-Verlag, 1986.

Bevan, David L.; Collier, Paul; and Gunning, Jan W. "Anatomy of a Temporary Trade Shock: The Kenya Coffee Boom of 1976-9". *Journal of African Economies* 1 (1992): 271-305.

-------------------------------------------------. *Controlled Open Economies: A Neoclassical Approach to Structuralism*. Oxford: Oxford University Press, 1990.

-------------------------------------------------."Fiscal Responses to a Temporary Terms of Trade Shock: The Aftermath of the Kenyan Coffee Boom". *World Bank Economic Review* 3 (September 1989): 359-78.

Bigsten, Arne. *Education and Income Distribution in Kenya*. Aldershot: Gower, 1984.

Blejer, Mario I., and Khan, Mohsin. "Government Policy and Private Investment in Developing Countries". *International Monetary Fund Staff Papers* 32 (June 1984): 379-403.

Blinder, Alan S., and Deaton, Angus. "The Time Series Consumption Function Revisited". *Brookings Papers on Economic Activity* 0(2) (1985): 465-511.

Branson, William H. "Stabilization Stagflation and Investment Incentives: The Case of Kenya, 1975-1980". In *Economic Adjustments and Exchange Rates in Developing Countries*. Sebastian Edwards and L. Ahmed, eds. Chicago: University of Chicago Press, 1986.

Bruno, Michael. "Adjustment and Structural Change Under Raw Material Price Shocks". *Scandinavian Journal of Economics* 84 (1982): 199-222.

-------------------. "Stabilization and Stagflation in a Semi Industrialized Economy". In *International Economic Policy: Theory and Evidence*. Rudiger Dornbusch and Jacob A. Frenkel, eds. Baltimore: Johns Hopkins University Press, 1979.

Bruno, Michael, and Sachs, Jeffrey, D. *Economics of World Wide Stagflation*. Cambridge, Mass.: Harvard University Press, 1985.

Buffie, Edward F. "Imported Inputs, Real Wage Rigidity and Devaluation in the Small Open Economy". *European Economic Review* 33 (1989): 1345-1361.

Chenery, Hollis B., and Srinivasan, Thirukodikaval, eds. *Handbook of Development Economics*. Amsterdam: North Holland, vol. I, 1988; vol. II, 1989.

Collier, Paul, and Lal, Deepak. *Labour and Poverty in Kenya, 1900-1980*. New York: Oxford University Press, 1986.

Conway, Patrick. *Economic Shocks and Structural Adjustments: Turkey After 1973*. Amsterdam: Elsevier Science Publishing Co., 1987.

------------------. "Decomposing the Determinants of Trade Deficits: Turkey in the 1970s". *Journal of Development Economics* 21 (May 1986): 235-259.

Coughlin, Peter, and Ikiara, Gerrishon, K. *Industrialization in Kenya: In Search of a Strategy*. Nairobi: Heinemann, 1988.

Deaton, Angus. "Savings in Developing Countries". *Proceedings of the World Bank Conference on Development Economics*. Stanley Fischer and Dennis de Tray, eds. Washington, DC: The World Bank (1989): 61-108.

----------------. "Life Cycle Models of Consumption: Is Evidence Consistent with Theory?". In *Advances in Econometrics: Fifth World Congress*. Truman F. Bewley, ed. Cambridge: Cambridge University Press, 1987.

Dervis, Kemal, and de Melo, Jaime. *General Equilibrium Models for Development Policy*. Cambridge: Cambridge University Press, 1982.

Dervis, Kemal; de Melo, Jaime; and Robinson, Sherman. "The Foreign Exchange Gap, Growth and Industrial Strategy in Turkey: 1973-1983". *Staff Working Paper* no. 306. Washington, D.C.: The World Bank, 1978.

Dick, Hermann; Gupta, Sanjeev; and Mayer, Thomas. "The Short-Run Impact of Fluctuating Primary Commodity Prices on Three Developing Economies: Colombia, Ivory Coast and Kenya". *World Development* 11 (May 1983): 405-416.

Dickey, David A., and Fuller, Wayne A. "Distribution of the Estimates for Regressive Time Series with a Unit Root". *Journal of the American Statistical Association* 74 (1979): 427-431.

Dolado, Juan; Jenkinson, Tim; and Simon, Sosvilla-Rivero. "Cointegration and Unit Roots". *Journal of Economic Surveys* 3 (1990): 249-273.

Dornbusch, Rudiger. "Exchange Rates and Monetary Policy in a Popular Model of International Trade". *American Economic Review* 65 (1975): 859-71.

Edwards, Sebastian. "Disequilibrium and Structural Adjustment". In Chenery and Srinivasan (1989).

Edwards, Sebastian. "Temporary Terms of Trade Disturbances, the Real Exchange Rate; and the Current Account". *Economica* 56 (August 1989): 343-357.

Engle, Robert F. "Autoregressive Conditional Heteroscedasticity with Estimates of the Variance of U.K. Inflation". *Econometrica* 50 (July 1982): 987-1007.

Faini, Riccardo, and Jaime de Melo. "Adjustment, Investment, and the Real Exchange Rate in Developing Countries". *Economic Policy* 5 (October 1990): 491-519.

Flavin, Marjorie A., "The Adjustment of Consumption to changing Expectations about Future Income". *Journal of Political Economy* 89 (1981): 974-1009.

Friedman, Benjamin, and Hahn, Frank, eds. *Handbook of Monetary Economics*. Amsterdam: North Holland, 1990.

Friedman, James W. *Game Theory with Applications in Economics*. New York: Oxford University Press, 1986.

Friedman, Milton. *A Theory of the Consumption Function*. Princeton, N.J.: Princeton University Press, 1957.

Gavin, Michael. "Structural Adjustment to a Terms of Trade Disturbance: The Role of Relative Prices". *Journal of International Economics* 28 (May 1990): 217-244.

Gersovitz, Mark. "Saving and Development". In Chenery and Srinivasan (1988).

Goldstein, Morris; Khan, Mohsin S.; and Officer, Lawrence O. "Prices of Tradable and Non-Tradable Goods in the Demand for Total Imports". *Review of Economics and Statistics* 62 (1980): 190-99.

Gulhati, Ravi, and Yalamanchili, S. "Contemporary Policy Responses to Economic Decline in Africa". *World Bank Report Series* no.439. Washington, D.C.: The World Bank, 1988.

Gulhati, Ravi; Swadish, Bose R.; and Vimal, Atukorala. "Exchange Rate Policies in Eastern and Southern Africa, 1965-83". *Staff Working Paper* no. 720. Washington, D.C.: The World Bank, 1984.

Gupta, Sanjeev and Togan, Subidey. "Who Benefits From The Adjustment Process in Developing Countries? A Test on India, Kenya, and Turkey". *Journal of Policy Modelling* 6 (1984): 95-109.

Hall, Robert, E. "Stochastic Implications Of the Permanent Income Hypothesis: Theory and Evidence". *Journal of Political Economy* 6 (December 1978): 971-86.

Hall, Robert E., and Jorgenson, Dale W. "Applications of the Theory of Optimal Capital Accumulation". In *Tax Incentives and Capital Spending. Brookings Conference on the Effects of Tax Policy on Investment*, Washington, D.C.: The Brookings Institution, 1967.

Hallwood, Paul, and MacDonald, Ronald. *International Money: Theory, Evidence and Institutions*. Oxford: Basil Blackwell, 1986.

Hansen, Lars, P., and Singleton, Kenneth. "Generalized Instrumental Variables Estimation of Rational Expectations Models". *Econometrica* 50 (September 1982): 1269-86.

Haque, Nadeem U., and Montiel, Peter J. "Dynamic Responses to Policy and Exogenous Shocks in an Empirical Developing-Country Model with Rational Expectations". *Economic Modelling* 8 (April 1991): 201-18.

------------------------------------------."Consumption in Developing Countries. Tests for Liquidity Constraints and Finite Horizons". *Review of Economics and Statistics* 71 (August 1989): 408-15.

Haque, Nadeem U., Lahiri, Kajal, and Montiel, Peter J. "A Macroeconometric Model for Developing Countries". *International Monetary Fund Staff Papers* 37 (September 1990): 537-59.

Harberger, Arnold C. "Currency Depreciation, Income and the Balance of Trade". *Journal of Political Economy* 58 (February 1950): 47-60.

Hayashi, Fumio. "Tests for Liquidity Constraints: A Critical Survey and Some New Observations". In *Advances in Econometrics: Fifth World Conference II*, Truman F. Brewely, ed. Cambridge: Cambridge University Press, 1985.

------------------. "Tobin's Marginal q and average q: A Neoclassical Interpretation". *Econometrica* 50 (January 1982): 213-224.

Hazlewood, Arthur. *The Economy of Kenya: The Kenyatta Era*. London: Oxford University Press, 1979.

Helpman, Elhanan, and Razin, Assaf. "The Role of Saving and Investment in Exchange Rate Determination, Under Alternative Monetary Rate Mechanisms". *Journal of Monetary Economics* 13 (May 1984): 307-25.

Ikiara, Gerrishon, K. "Structural Changes in The Kenyan Economy". In Killick (1981).

International Monetary Fund. *International Financial Statistics*. Washington. Various Issues.

International Labor Office. *Employment, Incomes and Inequality: A Strategy for Increasing Productive Employment in Kenya*. Geneva: The ILO, 1972.

Johnson, Harry G. "Towards a Theory of the Balance of Payments". In *International Trade and Economic Growth*, Harry G. Johnson. London: Allen and Unwin (1958).

Jorgenson, Dale W. "Capital Theory and Investment Behaviour". *American Economic Review Papers and Proceedings* 53 (May 1963): 247-259.

------------------. "The Theory of Investment Behaviour". In *Determinants of Investment Behaviour*, by R. Ferber. Washington D.C.: National Bureau of Economics Research, 1967.

Kalecki, Michal. *Selected Essays on the Dynamics of the Capitalist Economy*. London: Cambridge University Press, 1971.

Khan, Mohsin and Knight, Malcolm. "Determinants of Current Account Balance in Non-Oil Developing Countries in the 1970s: An Empirical Analysis". *International Monetary Fund Staff Papers* 30 (December 1983): 819-842.

Killick, Tony, ed. *The IMF and Stabilisation: Developing Country Experiences*. New York: St. Martins Press, 1984.

------------------, ed. *Papers on the Kenyan Economy: Performance, Problems and Policies*. Nairobi: Heinemann, 1981.

Killick, Tony, and Thorne, Maurice. "Problems of An Open Economy: The Balance of Payments in The Nineteen Seventies". In Killick (1981).

King, John Rawnsley. *Stabilization Policy in an African Setting: Kenya: 1963-1973*. London: Heinemann, 1979.

Krepps, David M. *A Course in Microeconomic Theory*. Princeton: Princeton University Press, 1990.

Krueger, Anne. *Turkey: Foreign Trade Regimes and Economic Development*. New York: National Bureau of Economic Research, 1974.

Krugman, Paul, and Taylor, Lance. "Contractionary Effects of Devaluation". *Journal of International Economics* 8 (August 1978): 445-56.

Lal, Deepak. *The Poverty of Development Economics*. Cambridge: Harvard University Press, 1986.

Laursen, Svend, and Metzler, Lloyd, A. "Flexible Exchange Rates and The Theory of Employment". *Review of Economics and Statistics* 32 (November 1950): 281-99.

Lewis, Jeffrey D., and Urata, Shujiro. "Anatomy of a Balance of Payments Crisis: Application of a Computable General Equilibrium Model to Turkey, 1978-1980". *Economic Modelling* 1 (July 1984): 281-305.

Lewis, Arthur W. "Economic Development With Unlimited Supplies of Labor". *The Manchester School* 22 (May 1954): 139-91.

Lucas, Robert E. "Econometric Policy Evaluation: A Critique". In *The Phillips Curve and Labor Markets*. Karl Brunner and Allan H. Meltzer, eds. Amsterdam: North Holland, 1976.

MacKinnon, Ronald "Critical Values for Cointegration Tests". *Working Paper*. San Diego: University of California, 1990.

Maitha, Joseph K.; Killick, Tony; and Ikiara, Gerrishon K. *The Balance of Payments Process in Developing Countries: Kenya*. Nairobi: University of Nairobi, 1978.

Maitha, Joseph K. and Manundu, Musembi. "Production Techniques, Factor Proportions, and Elasticities of Substitution". In Killick (1981).

Malinvaud, Edmond. "Wages and Unemployment". *Economics Journal* 92 (March 1982): 1-12.

Marion, Nancy P., and Svensson, Lars E.O. "World Equilibrium and Oil Price: An Intertemporal Analysis". *Oxford Economic Papers* 36 (1984): 86-102.

# Bibliography

Marion, Nancy P., and Svensson, Lars E.O. "Structural Differences and Macroeconomic Adjustment to Oil Price Increases in a Three Country Model". *Working Paper no. 839*, National Bureau of Economic Research, 1982.

Martson, R. C., and Turnovsky, S.J. "Imported Material Prices, Wage Policy and Macroeconomic Stabilization". *Working Paper no. 1254*. Cambridge, Mass.: National Bureau of Economic Research, December 1983.

Mitra, Pradeep. "Adjustment to External Shocks in Selected Semi-Industrial Countries, 1974-1981". *Discussion Paper no. 114*. Washington, D.C.: The World Bank, 1984.

Modigiliani, Franco, and Brumberg, R.E. "Utility Analysis and the Consumption Function". In *Post-Keynesian Economics*, Kenneth Kurihara, ed. New Brunswick, N. J.: Rutgers University Press, 1954.

Muet, Pierre-Allain. "Econometric Models of Investment: A Comparative Study On Annual Data". In *Investment and Factor Demand*, P. Artus and Pierre-Allain Muet eds. Amsterdam: North Holland, 1990.

Mukui, J. "Inflation in Kenya". Unpublished, University Of Nairobi, 1978.

Mundell, Robert. "The Monetary Dynamics of International Adjustment Under Fixed and Flexible Exchange Rates". *Quarterly Journal of Economics* 74 (1960): 227-57.

Mussa, Michael. "The Two sector Model In Terms of Its Dual". *Journal of International Economics* 9 (November 1979): 513-26.

Ndegwa, Phillip. *Report and Recommendations of the Working Party on Government Expenditures*. Nairobi: Government Printer, 1982.

Nigam, Ashok, and Handa, Jagdish. *Devaluation Policy and the Indian Economy*. New Delhi: S. Chand and Co., 1990.

Obstfeld, Maurice. "Aggregate Spending and The terms of Trade: Is there

147

a Laursen-Metzler Effect?" *Quarterly Journal of Economics* 97 (May 1982): 251-70.

Ostry, Jonathan D. "The Balance of Trade, Terms of Trade, and the Real Exchange Rate: An Intertemporal Optimizing Framework". *International Monetary Fund Staff Papers* 35 (December 1988): 541-73.

Pagan, Adrian R. "Econometric Issues in The Analysis of Regressions With Generated Regressors". *International Economic Review* 25: (Feb. 1984):221-47.

Pagan, Adrian R., and Wickens, Michael R., "A Survey of Recent Econometric Methods". *Economic Journal* 99 (December 1989): 962-1025.

Pindyck, Robert S. "Irreversibility, Uncertainty, and Investment". *Working Papers*. Washington, D.C.: The World Bank, 1989. Also published in *Journal of Economic Literature* 29 (Sept. 1991): 1110-48.

Polak, Jacques J. "Monetary Analysis of Income Formation and Payments Problems". *International Monetary Fund Staff Papers* 6 (November 1957): 1-50.

Ranis, Gustav, and Fei, John C.H. "A Theory of Economic Development". *American Economic Review* 51 (September 1961): 533-65.

Raut, Lakshmi K., and Virmani, Arvind. "Determinants of Consumption and Savings Behaviour in Developing Countries". *World Bank Economic Review* 3 (September 1989): 379-393.

Razin, Assaf. "Capital Movements, Intersectoral Resource Shifts, and the Trade Balance". *Seminar Paper no. 159*. Stockholm: Institute of International Economics Studies, University of Stockholm, 1980.

Republic of Kenya. *Development Plans*. Various Issues. Nairobi: Government Printer.

Robinson, Sherman. "Multisectoral Models of Developing Countries: A Survey". In Chenery and Srinivasan (1989).

Rossi, Nicolla. "Government Spending, the Real Interest Rate, and the Behaviour of Liquidity Constrained Consumers in Developing Countries". *International Monetary Fund Staff Papers* 35 (March 1988): 104-140.

Sachs, Jeffrey D. "The Current Account in The Macroeconomic Adjustment Process". *Scandinavian Journal of Economics* 84 (1982): 147-59.

----------------. "The Current Account and Macroeconomic Adjustment in 1970s". *Brookings Papers on Economic Activity* 1 (1981): 201-68.

Sharpley, Jennifer. "Resource Transfers Between the Agricultural Sector and Non-Agricultural Sectors: 1964-1977". In Killick (1981).

Sgro, Pasquale M. *The Theory of Duality and International Trade*. London: Croom Helm, 1986.

Solimano, Andrea. "How Investment Responds to Changing Macroeconomic Conditions: The case of Chile in the 1980s". *Working Papers*. Washington: The World Bank, 1989.

Spanos, Aris. *Statistical Foundations of Economic Modelling*. Cambridge: Cambridge University Press, 1989.

Svensson, Lars E.O. "Oil Prices and a Small Oil Producing Country's Welfare and the Trade Balance: An Intertemporal Approach". *Seminar Paper no. 184*. Stockholm: Institute of International Economic Studies, University of Stockholm, 1981.

Svensson, Lars E.O., and Razin, Assaf. "The Terms of Trade and the Current Account: The Harberger-Laursen-Metzler Effect". *Journal of Political Economy* 91 (February 1983): 97-125.

Taylor, Lance. *Structuralist Macroeconomics*. New York: Basic Books, 1983.

Tobin, James. "A General Equilibrium Approach to Monetary Theory". *Journal of Money, Credit and Banking* 1 (February 1969): 5-29.

------------------. *Stabilization and Growth in Developing Countries: A Structuralist Approach*. New York: Harwood Academic Publishers, 1989.

Vandermortelle, Jan. "Causes of Economic Instability in Kenya: Theory and Evidence". *East African Economic Review* 1 (December 1986): 81-96.

------------------. "Kenya Data Compendium 1964-1982". *Occasional Paper No. 44*. Nairobi: Institute for Development Studies, University of Nairobi, 1985.

Varian, Hal. *Microeconomic Analysis*. New York: W.W. Norton, 1984.

Wickens, Richard M. "The Efficient Estimation of Econometric Models with Rational Expectations". *Review of Economic Studies* 49 (January 1982): 56-67.

Woodland, Alan. *International Trade and Resource Allocation*. Amsterdam: North Holland, 1982.

World Bank. *World Tables*. London: Johns Hopkins University Press, 1989 and 1990.

------------------. *Accelerated Development in Sub-Saharan Africa*. Baltimore: Johns Hopkins University Press, 1980.

------------------. *Kenya: Into the Second Decade*. Baltimore: Johns Hopkins University Press, 1975.

Zagame, P. "L'Investissement En Desequilibre". In *Economie du Desequilibre*, edited by C. de Boissieu, A. Parguez, and P. Zagame. Paris: Economica, 1977.

# Bibliography

Zuelhke, Thomas W., and James, E. Payne. "Tests of the Rational Expectations Permanent Income Hypothesis for Developing Economies". *Journal of Macroeconomics* 11 (Summer 1989): 423-33.

# DATE DUE